Cycling the
Trans Pennine Trail

Cycling the Trans Pennine Trail

Nicolas Mitchell

THE CROWOOD PRESS

First published in 2015 by The Crowood Press, The Stable Block, Crowood Lane, Ramsbury, Marlborough, Wiltshire SN8 2HR

enquiries@crowood.com
www.crowood.com
This impression 2022

Text copyright ©2014 Nicolas Mitchell
All photographs are by the author, unless specified otherwise

Nicolas Mitchell hereby asserts and gives notice of his right to be identified under Sections 77 and 78 of the Copyright, Designs and Patents Act 1988, as the author of this work. All rights reserved. No part of this work may be reproduced, stored in a retrieval system, or transmitted in any form or by any means, electronic, mechanical, photocopying, recording or otherwise, without the prior permission of the publishers.

About the Author

Nicolas Mitchell is passionate about cycle touring. He has thousands of cycling miles to his credit and is a veteran of numerous long-distance cycle rides. This book explores the Trans Pennine Trail, a route growing in popularity. When he isn't in the office writing up cycling routes, Nicolas can usually be found out on the road guiding long-distance cycle tours.

Every effort has been made to ensure the accuracy of this book. However, changes can occur during the lifetime of an edition. The Publishers cannot be held responsible for any errors or omissions or for the consequences of any reliance on the information given in this book. We advise readers to check such things as accommodation and transport before setting out to cycle the Trans Pennine Trail.

As with any outdoor activity, accidents and injury can occur. The Publishers accept no responsibility for any injuries which may occur in relation to using or following the route described, or the information contained within this book.

Frontispiece: Sustrans volunteers at work on the Trans Pennine Trail. (Photo: Nicolas Mitchell)

ISBN: 978 1 84797 875 2

Typeset by Servis Filmsetting Ltd, Stockport, Cheshire
Printed in India by Parksons Graphics Pvt Ltd

CONTENTS

FOLLOWING THE TRAIL	6
INTRODUCTION	9
ESSENTIALS	12
NAVIGATION	12
NUTRITION AND FITNESS	13
WHEN TO GO AND WHAT BICYCLE TO TAKE	20
WHAT GEAR TO TAKE	20
TRAVEL	21
STAGE 1: SOUTHPORT TO LYMM	22
MANCHESTER SHIP CANAL	39
STAGE 2: LYMM TO WENTWORTH CASTLE	42
THE LONGDENDALE VALLEY	55
WOODHEAD TUNNEL	60
STAGE 3: WENTWORTH CASTLE TO SELBY	72
DEARNE VALLEY RSPB OLD MOOR NATURE RESERVE	75
CONISBROUGH CASTLE	78
CONISBROUGH VIADUCT	80
RAF BURN	87
SELBY ABBEY	89
STAGE 4: SELBY TO HORNSEA	92
HUMBER BRIDGE	100
RESOURCES	109
INDEX OF VILLAGES, TOWNS AND LANDMARKS	144

FOLLOWING THE TRAIL

The book is divided into six sections. The Essentials section deals with preparation and gives advice on navigation, type of bike, what to take, what to eat, what to wear, weather conditions and getting to and from start and finish points. The next four sections of the book comprise the route description of stages 1-4 of the Trans Pennine Trail. The final section is Resources, which includes a list of places to stay to suit different budgets, cycle repair shops and mechanics along the way, transport information and also useful websites.

STAGES

Each stage section is colour coded and opens with an overview map, a description of the terrain, distance covered and OS maps required. The route description includes a complete series of grid references to aid navigation. There are also features on the flora and fauna encountered on the route, fascinating insights into the industrial heritage of the area plus full-colour and archive photography to illustrate the main points of interest.

MAPS AND ELEVATION PROFILES

There are twenty-five maps covering each stage of the 205-mile route, plus five elevation profiles showing the height gain and loss (in metres) along each stage of the route. As well as the route, the maps also show public houses and cafes recommended for a stop and points of interest along the way.

ELEVATION PROFILE OF TRANS PENNINE TRAIL

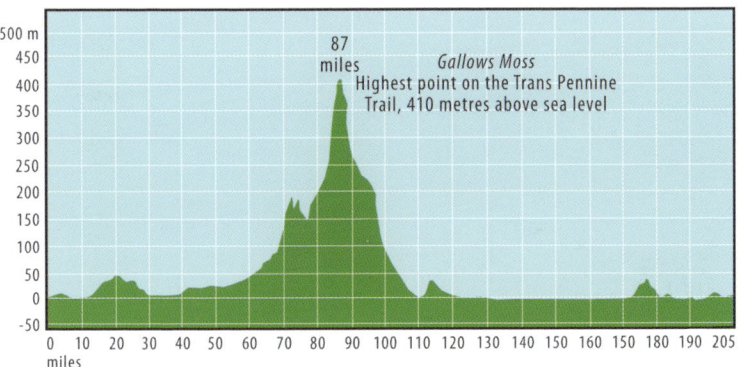

KEY TO MAPS

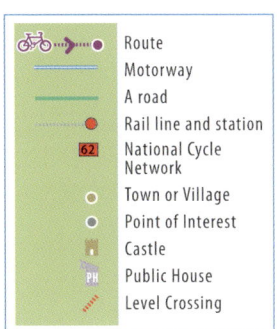

A poem in honour of the Trans Pennine Trail

Shining light from East to West,
Link from sea to sea.
Tightrope walk across the North
Bringing you to me.

Following the sun across the sky
From Dawn to evening sea;
Lifeline, heartline on the hand of The North
Bringing you to me.

Summer, Autumn, Winter, Spring
Seasons turn from sea to sea.
Frozen puddles, baking track
Bringing you to me.

Celebrate the Trans Pennine Trail
Open your eyes to see
A plan, a dream, a walk, a ride
Through urban sites and countryside
A source of country-crossing pride
Bringing you to me:
Here's to the TPT!

This poem is reproduced with the kind permission of Ian McMillan and was specially written by Ian for the Trans Pennine Trail to launch the eastern terminus Seamark at Hornsea on 20 October 2003 © Ian McMillan.

INTRODUCTION

The Trans Pennine Trail (TPT) is one of the finest long-distance cycle rides in England. Tackling the route over four days is a marvellous mini-adventure that should appeal to all sorts of cyclists from the newcomer, to long-distance tours, through to the 'roadie' looking for something different. The TPT route described in this book is approximately 205 miles long and it starts on the seafront close to Pleasureland in Southport, Merseyside. It progresses through Aintree, into Liverpool, to the south of Manchester and the north of Sheffield, traversing Doncaster, Selby, Hull and then finally out to Hornsea, a small seaside town in the East Riding of Yorkshire. It is sensational, combining some of the very best urban cycling and some fantastic 'big sky' riding as the route pushes north towards Selby and onto Hull and Hornsea.

The base of the Seamark obelisk. (Photo: Terry Eaton, Eaton Waygood Associates)

Introduction

The TPT may lack the instant recognition of Lands End to John O'Groats. It doesn't boast the consistently spectacular moorland scenery associated with the Sea-to-Sea or Way of the Roses nor the unfolding drama of the Coast and Castles. Yet the TPT has a character all of its own. It is predominantly off-road. It is brimming with traces of the Industrial Revolution and it offers a glorious opportunity to explore the natural history of England in some very surprising locations.

In 2006 the TPT won the coveted Amazing Space award presented by the National Lottery for the remarkable manner in which the trail makes innovative use of the trackbeds of disused railway lines and canal towpaths. These former trading arteries which pierce the towns and great cities of the North were revitalized and transformed with an investment of around £30 million before the TPT was officially opened in 2001, giving the keen leisure cyclist the chance to ride for miles without coming into contact with motor vehicles.

As you progress from the Irish Sea to the North Sea you will encounter areas where Romans and kings, Victorian industrialists and gifted civil engineers have all left their mark. For those cyclists who enjoy natural history, the TPT traverses numerous nature reserves, including Pickerings Pasture, Reddish Vale and RSPB Old Moor, to name just three. Overall the topography of the ride is relatively flat, played out on traffic-free cycle paths and country lanes. There is one significant climb which begins after approximately 80 miles (Stage Two) with a steady ascent from Hadfield along the Longdendale Trail to the Woodhead Tunnel. From the Woodhead Tunnel there is a short, steep ascent onto Gallows Moss at 1,372 feet above sea level, followed by a long exhilarating descent into Dunford Bridge.

This book has been designed to act as a guide and an aid to riding the length of the TPT from west to east over four days. It is divided into a number of short sections which cover navigation, fitness and nutrition. The guide highlights when to go and what gear to take and includes a kit list. We have also devoted a short section within the book dealing with bicycle transport. This should be useful when planning your arrival at the start point and your departure after successfully completing the ride. Within the main section of the book, each stage of the ride is fully described and you will find sketch plans of the route and elevation graphs throughout. The sketch plans contained within each stage have been designed so that they are naturally orienteered to the direction of travel.

In addition to the practical details of the ride there are a number of vignettes which relate to points of interest along the route, such as the Manchester Ship Canal, Conisbrough Castle and Selby Abbey. There is also some information on the various species of birds that you may see along the Longdendale Trail and

Introduction

The TPT signboard.

a more detailed introduction to the RSPB centre at Old Moor in the Dearne Valley, one of the outstanding locations of the TPT.

Towards the end of the book you will find a list of resources, including tourist information websites that cover the TPT and a comprehensive list of accommodation arranged geographically from west to east. There is a list of bicycle repair shops, mobile bicycle mechanics and more general cycling links. The reader will find an 'at a glance guide' to the key villages, towns and landmarks, which will help when setting up electronic navigational tools. We are confident that through this combination of practical advice, route description and the information contained in the Resources section, the budding adventurer should have all the tools required for an exciting and rewarding cycle tour along the TPT.

ESSENTIALS

NAVIGATION

One of the outstanding features of the TPT is that the route is extensively signed from start to finish. The signs are well designed, clear and numerous, and it is quite straightforward to cycle the entire 205 miles relying entirely on the sketch plans within this guide and the National Cycle Network (NCN) and TPT signposts.

For those riders who enjoy more detailed planning and navigating, then mapping will be an important aspect of your tour preparations. We believe that the most suitable maps for cycle touring are the Ordnance Survey Landranger series 1:50,000. This scale fits perfectly with the rhythm of long-distance cycling at a steady pace of anything from 10 to 14 miles per hour. They include just enough detail but not too much. You will need seven Landranger maps to complete the TPT and full details are listed under Resources at the back of the book. You should be able to save money by borrowing the maps from your local library. Alternatively you may find second-hand copies on eBay for a pound or two.

Navigating with a physical map on your handlebars is great fun and very rewarding. For those riders who enjoy this aspect of touring we have included every significant turning and junction as a grid reference throughout the body of the book; these references are denoted by two letters followed by six digits for example SD 326 175, SJ 895 908, etc. It should be a simple matter to transfer the references from the book and plot the route onto the Landrangers before commencing the ride. Additionally, grid references are used to mark the location of hotels, bed and breakfast accommodation, youth hostels and cycle repair shops. If you are a little unsure about how to plot a grid reference onto a Landranger map, Robert B. Matkin's book *Map Reading* (ISBN 978-1855680968), published by Dalesman in 2008, is a very user-friendly introduction.

With the revolution in information technology, many riders will choose to navigate the TPT using a Global Positioning System, smartphone or tablet rather than a traditional paper map. To do this you will need an open source mapping application. There are some excellent free resources on the internet and we believe that the best is Google Maps. Since September 2012 there is also an iPhone app for Google Maps, although Open Street Map, Garmin Basecamp, Ordnance Survey OS Open Data are all tremendous resources. You may also find the National Cycle Network app from Sustrans and their online mapping

Essentials

of the National Cycle Network very helpful. Many cyclists who have already completed the TPT have uploaded their routes and maps to the cycling website Map My Ride and it is quite easy to download the GPX files from this resource directly to your computer, GPS, smartphone, etc. Finally the website nearby.org.uk will convert a grid reference or postcode into a physical location onto a host of open source mapping resources such as emapsite.com, Streetmap or Magic Defra. This should prove invaluable when searching for a bed and breakfast, youth hostel or cycle shop.

NUTRITION AND FITNESS

You do not need to be super-fit to complete the TPT nor will you need to prepare for weeks with a specially designed diet, but giving some general thought to your fitness and what you eat before, during and after each day on the bicycle will make the whole TPT experience more enjoyable. In this section of the book we want to try and help our readers with nutrition and fitness. It hardly needs saying that you will need to be in robust health before attempting the TPT. Although not the toughest ride in the pantheon of long-distance cycle tours, the TPT can still deliver a surprise, especially on the climb to Gallows Moss. With this in mind we recommend that you visit your General Practitioner for a health check-up before undertaking the ride.

With regard to fitness, there are some excellent resources on the web which will help you personalize your training plan. One of the best is Do It For Charity, where you will find a section on the website dedicated to cycling fitness. The British Heart Foundation has also produced a clear and concise beginner's fitness programme. We believe that there is no substitute for being out and about on your bicycle. If possible make it your preferred mode of transport, use it for commuting or going to the shops, and you will soon build up some cycling fitness. Around two weeks before the start of the TPT try and do two consecutive days of around 20 to 30 miles in the saddle. If you have never undertaken a long-distance ride before, this is a good way of assessing your general fitness whilst giving you a little extra time to get a final few miles under your belt. The best cycling fitness books and websites we could find are listed at the back of this book.

Long-distance cycle touring can be divided into four key elements. These are route preparation, equipment (bicycle and clothing), fitness, and finally nutrition. It is a great feeling to undertake a challenge and know that you are very well prepared. We work with many cyclists who are passionate about their sport. They have the finest GPS devices, they invest thousands of pounds on their

Essentials

A colourful selection of healthy cycling food. (Photo: Wikimedia Commons)

bicycles and cycling kit. These dedicated riders will religiously go out into the hills on training rides yet they give little, if any, thought to their cycling diet. In this short section we want to highlight why nutrition is a very important aspect of preparation for and execution of a long-distance cycling tour such as the TPT. It is vital that you have the stamina and endurance to complete the ride. Running out of energy 6 miles before arriving at your hotel in the dark will make the TPT memorable for all the wrong reasons.

A good place to start your nutritional preparation is to adopt a healthy balanced diet for everyday living and the National Health Service website gives some sound advice. All that remains is to decide what to eat during the course of the adventure. Without becoming too technical we have highlighted foods with a low, medium and high glycaemic index (GI). The GI ranks food and fluids

Essentials

by how carbohydrate-rich they are and how quickly they affect the body's blood sugar levels. This is important on the TPT. You should look for a slow release of energy, especially for breakfast and for your evening meal. With this in mind, try to choose foods with a low GI. For a short burst of energy choose a food source with a high GI. The paragraphs below give an indication of the GI of common carbohydrates.

Low GI: Legumes such as beans (kidney, white, black, pink and soy) and nuts (almonds, peanuts, walnuts and chickpeas). Seeds (sunflower, flax, pumpkin, poppy and sesame), most vegetables (beets and parsnips) and most intact grains (durum, wheat, millet, oat, rye, rice and barley) as well as honey, muesli, sweet corn, kiwi fruit, banana, baked beans, peas, carrots, grapes, apples, pears, plain low fat yoghurt, rye bread, boiled potato, spaghetti, barley, orange, lentils, skimmed milk, and peanuts.

Medium GI: Pitta bread, basmati rice, potato, grape juice, raisins, prunes, cranberry juice, croissant, instant porridge, raisins, rye crispbread, muesli bar, pizza, porridge, pineapple, sultanas, Rich Tea biscuit, oatmeal biscuit, couscous, Power Bar, sweet potato, ice cream.

High GI: Dates, white bread, most white rice, cornflakes, potatoes, baked potato, mashed potato, chips, Weetabix, watermelon, Rice Krispies, bagel, Bran Flakes, Cheerios.

With the help of nutritionist Ann Sinclair of Nutribox, we have designed a very simple menu, which will give you some ideas as to what to eat when you are cycling the TPT. It is very important to drink plenty of water – staying hydrated is critical. Ideally aim to drink one to one and a half litres of water per day and drink more if you feel particularly thirsty. Under Resources at the back of this book, you will find a number of online and hard copy resources regarding nutrition.

Breakfast
Cornflakes or other cereal with nuts and/or seeds sprinkled on top
Milk or yoghurt
Porridge
Muesli
Beans on toast or scrambled eggs on toast
Banana or other fruit
Orange or other fruit or vegetable juice

Essentials

Lunch
Cheese and ham salad sandwich on brown bread
Boiled egg
Pasta and tuna salad
Apple
Yoghurt

Dinner
Basmati rice
Pasta
Fish, lean poultry or other lean meat
Selection of vegetables (try and aim for a broad range of colours every day)
Potatoes
Fresh fruit

Try to eat a variety of fresh fruit and vegetables every day. (Photo: Olerys, Frutase Vegetais/Wikimedia Commons)

Essentials

CYCLING SUPPERS

When you've been in the saddle all day you want a supper that is going to be ready quickly, is going to fill you up, and give you the important nutrition you need to restock your body for the next day. This means carbohydrate to replace all the glycogen you've burned up in your muscles, protein to support muscle repair, and don't forget taste – if you're not enjoying a meal you won't digest it as well and that means you won't get maximum nutritional value.

These four cycling suppers are designed to be quick and easy to make, with flexible ingredients so you can make use of what you can get hold of on the road.

1. CAMPING COOKER CASSOULET

Ingredients
(serves 2)
1 × 400g tinned tomatoes
1 × 400g tin of mixed pulses
1 medium onion (if you can get it)
Optional – whatever other vegetables you can get hold of, try carrots, courgettes, mushrooms; use tinned if necessary
4 × sausages

Method
In one pan start to cook the sausages, turning regularly – ensure they are fully cooked through before serving (time will depend on the size). In another pan fry the onion (if you have one); once softened add the tinned tomatoes, mixed pulses and any other vegetables being used. Leave the tomato, bean and vegetable mix to cook for 10 minutes or so, season to taste.

Serve your sausages on top of your tasty tomato stew for a cheat's version of the classic cassoulet!

This dish provides carbohydrate-rich vegetables as well as great protein and dietary fibre in the beans, and essential amino acids in the meat in the sausages. Tasty and filling, it will help you refuel for tomorrow.

Essentials

2. PANNIER PASTA

Ingredients
(serves 2)
100g dried pasta
1 x 200g (approx. 150g drained weight) tin salmon
200ml tub of crème fraiche *or* sour cream *or* natural yoghurt
Choice of vegetables – try one small tin of sweetcorn, peas or a small jar of roast peppers or sun dried tomatoes or artichoke hearts
1–2 tablespoons of tomato *or* chilli tomato ketchup (optional)

Method
In one pan bring water to the boil and put the pasta in to cook.
In a second pan heat the crème fraiche (or equivalent) with the vegetables and ketchup (if using).
When the pasta is ready, drain and stir into the sauce; season to taste.

The pasta in this dish will get your glycogen stores fully loaded again while the fat in the dairy sauce will help you feel full. It's important to get your five a day even when you're on the road so add as many portions of the vegetables as you can get hold of. The ketchup is optional but can provide a bit more flavour – and there's an important phytonutrient called lycopene which is more available from cooked tomatoes than raw.

3. ROAD CYCLER RICE

Ingredients
(serves 2)
1 x express rice, preferably whole grain (this is ready cooked rice which comes in pouches designed for use in a microwave, but you can heat the contents in a pan)
A healthy pinch of chilli flakes (optional – but gives it a nice kick!)
Vegetables – use a similar approach as for the pasta, using fresh, tinned or preserved vegetables depending on what you can get hold of
1 x 400g mixed pulses and/or 200g chicken or a small bag of frozen cooked prawns

Tips
You can often find packs of cooked chicken for snacking that work well in this recipe – and it saves you carrying and cooking raw meat.

Essentials

You can use whatever meat or other protein source you like in this dish – you can choose to include the beans *and* another source of protein, or just choose one, it's up to you. If you include the beans it will be more filling and give you more energy.

If you like your rice with a bit of sauce, use tomato or chilli ketchup, or tinned tomatoes – just add them into the mix and heat thoroughly.

Method
You can make this in just one pan – combine the rice, vegetables, pulses and/or meat in one pan.
Heat gently until all ingredients are piping hot; season to taste.
Note – if you're using raw meat, cook it first then add the other ingredients.

4. NEARLY NICOISE SALAD

Ingredients
(serves 2)
2 hard boiled eggs, chopped
250g new potatoes
1 x 200g (approx. 150g drained weight) tinned tuna and/or 4–6 rashers back bacon
100g fine green beans (tinned or fresh), chopped into 3–4cm pieces
2–3 tomatoes, chopped
Olive oil and the juice of one lemon (to dress the salad)

Method
In a pan hard boil the eggs then leave to cool – chop when cooled.
In another pan boil the potatoes until cooked, add the green beans for the last 3–4 mins of cooking (if using fresh rather than tinned).
Drain the potatoes and mix in all the other ingredients.
Drizzle 1–2 tablespoons of olive oil and the juice of one lemon to dress (or use a sachet of salad dressing if you prefer).
Season to taste and serve.

The potatoes in this salad provide a filling source of carbohydrate which will help restock your energy stores for tomorrow's cycling. The tuna and/or bacon will provide protein, and if you would prefer to substitute other vegetables for the green beans or add additional vegetables, feel free to do so. The more colours and different types of vegetables (or fruit) you add to this salad, the healthier it will be. © Ann Sinclair

Essentials

WHEN TO GO AND WHAT BICYCLE TO TAKE

The TPT can be undertaken at any time of the year although spring, summer and autumn are the most enjoyable. After heavy rain the TPT becomes muddy in places and, as it is a predominantly off-road ride, for that reason we strongly advise riders to undertake the 205-mile journey on a hybrid bike. To clarify, a hybrid bike is designed for light off-road touring. It is an ideal choice for the TPT and depending on the make and model it may or may not have front suspension. Ideally it should have 700cc wheels and wider tyres than you would find on a road bike. A hybrid bicycle, such as the one made by Bronx, retails at around £380, although there are bargains to be found on the internet and the classified advertisements of your local paper. As you can see, the Bronx is fitted with mudguards and a rear rack which will allow you to attach a pannier rather than carry a rucksack.

WHAT GEAR TO TAKE

On a long-distance cycle tour we believe that it is best to travel as lightly as you possibly can; the less gear you take, the easier the journey. Listed below are the essentials for riding the TPT at all times of year.

The Bronx hybrid bicycle. (Photo: Bronx Cycles)

Essentials

Hybrid bicycle
A single pannier that clips onto the back rack of a hybrid bicycle
Cycling helmet
High visibility tabard/vest
Waterproof jacket
Waterproof overtrousers
Waterproof overshoes
Trainers or cycling shoes
Cycling shorts (2)
Cycling shirts (2)
Fleece
Multi-tool
Puncture repair kit
Cable ties
Mobile phone
First aid kit
Pump
Front and rear lights
Reflector
Bell
Cyclocomputer
Camera
Sunglasses
Washing kit
Towel
Sun cream
Siopel or Neat 3B Action Cream – both are non-prescription products available at a local chemist and excellent for dealing with saddle sores.

TRAVEL

Aside from cycling, the most environmentally friendly way to arrive in Southport to start the TPT and to travel home after the conclusion of the ride is by train. A rule of thumb is to assume that bicycle reservations are required for most journeys on most trains. It is therefore essential that you reserve a space for your bicycle when booking your train ticket. Currently only East Coast trains offer an online facility where you can book a ticket and make a bicycle reservation in the same transaction. The National Rail website has some very useful information pertinent to the carriage of bicycles on trains.

At the conclusion of the ride the final matter to deal with is returning home. If you are returning to Hull immediately after completing the TPT, we have listed a number of taxi companies in the Resources section at the back of this book, which will transport cyclists and their bicycles from Hornsea back to Hull and other destinations. Once you have arrived in Hull there are frequent trains to Liverpool, Manchester and London Kings Cross as well as the usual connections to other cities and towns within the UK.

You may even consider travelling home by coach; National Express operates a regular service from Hull. They will carry bicycles on board; however, it appears that this service really only applies to boxed or folding bicycles. It is worth thoroughly checking their conditions of carriage before booking a ticket.

STAGE 1:

44.6 miles
Terrain: Flat

Maps required:
Ordnance Survey Landranger Sheet 108: Liverpool
Ordnance Survey Landranger Sheet 109: Manchester

SOUTHPORT TO LYMM

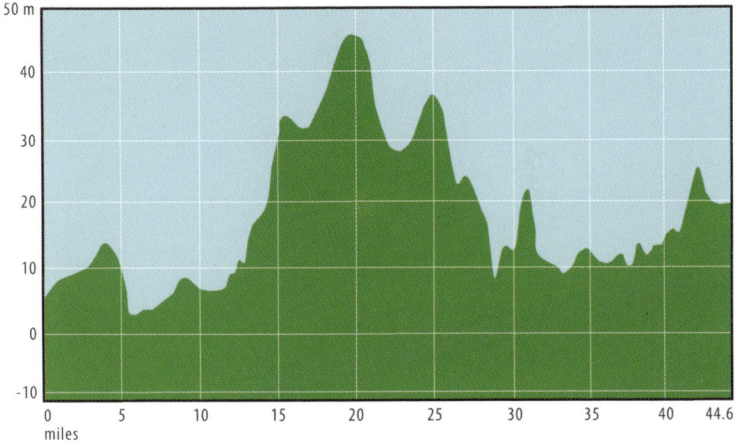

Starting any long-distance cycle ride can be a nervous and slightly stressful affair. To make the first day of the ride as enjoyable as possible we recommend arriving the night before the start of the adventure and staying in accommodation in Southport. This seaside town offers a whole host of accommodation to suit all tastes and budgets. This should find you refreshed and relaxed ready for the start. On the morning of the ride it is worth stocking up for lunch with sandwiches and fruit from Morrisons supermarket close to the start point. The official start of the TPT is from the Seamark (**SD 326 175**) Marine Drive, Southport, located on the southern end of the promenade close to the Pleasureland amusement and fairground complex.

As you pause and take the obligatory photographs before starting the ride, you will notice a range of sculptures, the most distinctive of which is the Seamark obelisk designed by Eaton Waygood Associates. The artworks along the seafront take their design inspiration from the sea, wind, tides, stars, the moon and the vast skies which give this area of Merseyside its own distinct character. The Seamark itself is topped with the TPT logo which rotates in the wind and is constructed from materials which were specifically chosen to reflect the light and maximize

Stage 1: Southport to Lymm

Pleasureland. (Photo: Nick Laister)

The first miles on the Trans Pennine Trail.

Stage 1: Southport to Lymm

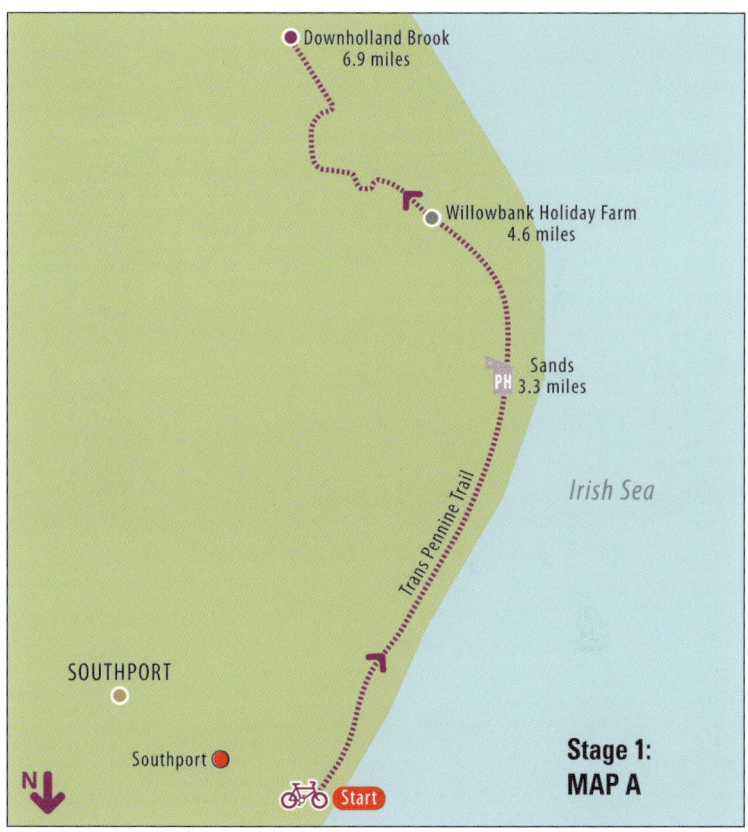

its visual effect. The Seamark is also designed to be seen from a distance and give a celebratory feeling to the start (or finish) of the journey. You will find an identical Seamark at Hornsea on the east coast.

For those riders who are using hard copy maps for navigation, the first map you will need to use is Ordnance Survey Landranger Sheet 108: Liverpool. You should commence the ride at the Seamark, Marine Drive, Southport, with the Irish Sea away to your right and follow the signs marked Ainsdale 25 minutes National Cycle Network (NCN) 62. Continue onwards for 3.3 miles to the Sands public house (**SD 302 128**), and then cycle along Coastal Road for a further 1.3 miles.

Stage 1: Southport to Lymm

After 4.6 miles from the start at the Seamark you will pass the entrance to Willowbank Holiday and Touring Park (**SD 311 109**). Continue for 0.3 miles to reach the junction of Coastal Road and the A565 Liverpool Road (**SD 312 107**) and go straight over into Moor Lane. This junction is 4.9 miles from the start. Having safely crossed the A565 Liverpool Road cycle along Moor Lane and into Plex Moss Lane and after 5.8 miles from the start at the Seamark you should turn right onto the TPT Cheshire Lines Path (**SD 326 102**).

The turning is marked by a signpost which highlights the historic role played by the Southport and Cheshire Lines Extension Railway (SCLR) in the area.

SOUTHPORT AND CHESHIRE LINES EXTENSION RAILWAY

The route from the Seamark at Southport utilizes the trackbed of this former railway line, forging a path towards Aintree. You may pause and wonder why a railway line would once pass through this quiet countryside. The answer lies in the expansion of the railways and a bid to profit from Southport's burgeoning tourist traffic and a growing local population. Around 130 years ago Southport was one of the premier seaside resorts in the country. It boasted a garden city design and was home to some fine shops and feted as the 'Montpellier of the North'. It attracted thousands of visitors and was a popular dormitory town for businessmen whose interests lay in nearby Liverpool and Manchester. In addition Southport's population was expanding rapidly: in the space of ten years it had increased from 18,000 to 46,000. These were halcyon days and the town's patriarchs were keen to exploit every commercial opportunity. Although well served by existing rail companies it was thought that another rail connection could only help the town prosper. In 1878 the first scheme to extend the line from Aintree to Southport was put before the existing Cheshire Lines Committee (CLC), who were an established, energetic and acquisitive railway company who already controlled a significant part of the rail network in Lancashire. The CLC agreed to support the extension of the line from Aintree out to Southport but they would not finance the venture.

With the tacit support – if not the monetary muscle – of the CLC behind them, the SCLR was formed in November 1880 to construct an extension of the existing railway line out from Aintree to Southport.

Stage 1: Southport to Lymm

The track bed of the former Cheshire Lines Committee railway line.

Financing the project proved difficult and construction of the new line was beset with delays and financial difficulties. Eventually the line opened for passenger traffic on 1 September 1884, running from Lord Street Station in Southport for 14 miles down to Aintree. From the very start the SCLR never did well. It faced stiff competition from other rail companies, which meant fewer passengers than originally forecast. This quickly brought matters to crisis point. Only four years after opening, the receivers had been called in and the line was only saved from bankruptcy and closure when the CLC stepped in to stabilize the finances and secure its long-term future. This rescue operation was formalized by an Act of Parliament whereby the SCLR extension would retain its separate identity but would be operated by the CLC in perpetuity. Despite the significant numbers of commuters and tourists travelling to and from Southport, the ever-present competition from its rivals meant that the line continued to struggle. In 1926 it was ridiculed by the press who dubbed it 'the never never railway'. The SCLR limped on until 1945, by which time there were only three stopping trains per day. The bright future for the line never materialized. By 1948 it was with a sense of relief that the line was nationalized and on 7 July 1952 it was closed.

Stage 1: Southport to Lymm

You should now continue along the old railway trackbed and after 6.9 miles from the Seamark you will cross Downholland Brook (**SD 327 087**). From there continue onwards on the NCN 62 and after approximately 11.9 miles you will emerge onto the B5422 Sefton Lane, Maghull (**SD 365 018**). At this junction look for the Optoplast Factory at the corner of Sefton Lane and Old Racecourse Road. Cycle along Old Racecourse Road on the NCN 62, go through an area of suburban housing (**SD 367 015**) and then into the splendid Jubilee Wood (**SD 366 009**), which was originally part of a landfill site. It was transformed into community woodland as part of the celebration of the Queen's Golden Jubilee.

The Forestry Commission have planted thousands of broad leaf and conifer-

Stage 1: Southport to Lymm

ous trees in the area, which were especially chosen to encourage red squirrels to the woodland. Having enjoyed the tranquil surroundings of Jubilee Wood, continue onwards on the NCN 62 into Chapel Lane and follow this road to its junction with the A5207 Northern Perimeter Road (**SD 359 003**). You should now be 13.2 miles from the start line at the Seamark in Southport. Cross the Northern Perimeter Road and continue onwards for 0.2 miles and then turn left (**SJ 359 999**) onto the towpath at the side of the Leeds Liverpool Canal. Cycle along the canal towpath for approximately 0.9 miles and leave the towpath via Wally's Steps (**SJ 370 991**) (you will see an NCN 62 sign for Liverpool) and turn right again following the sign indicating the TPT towards Liverpool 14½.

Stage 1: Southport to Lymm

West Derby railway station. (Photo: Martin Jones)

The former railway station at West Derby as it looks today.

Stage 1: Southport to Lymm

Continue on the NCN 62 cycling at the side of the A59 Ormskirk Road for 0.4 miles and then turn right into Heysham Road, where the Bathstore and Dreams bed superstore are easily recognized navigational waypoints. This junction is signed for the TPT NCN 62. Follow the signs for the NCN 62 as it weaves through an industrial area for 0.5 miles and at the junction of Park Lane and the A59 Ormskirk Road turn right (**SJ 366 978**), remaining on the NCN 62. At this point you should be approximately 15.3 miles from the start point at the Seamark in Southport. Aintree railway station and Aintree racecourse are useful navigational waypoints.

Having turned right onto Ormskirk Road, cycle past the Queens Arms public house and after 0.2 miles from the junction of Park Lane (Aintree racecourse) turn left into Melling Road. Cycle onwards for 0.1 miles and then turn right into Greenwich Road (**SJ 369 976**); at this point you will have cycled 15.6 miles from the Seamark, Southport. Cycle down Greenwich Road, go under a bridge and after approximately 250 yards turn left and continue along the TPT. This turning is easy to miss so we suggest that you pay particular attention. You will now be rewarded with around 5 miles of off-road urban cycling as the TPT follows the former Liverpool Loop Line through Walton, West Derby to Knotty Ash.

Sainsbury's at Knotty Ash (**SJ 403 914**) (112 East Prescot Road, Liverpool, Merseyside L14 5PT, tel. 0151 228 3262) is adjacent to the TPT (Liverpool Loop Line) and is a convenient location for a snack or lunch. The restaurant is open from 8am to 7pm Monday to Saturday and 10am to 3pm on Sundays. At this point you should be approximately 20.5 miles from the start at the Seamark, Southport.

You may wish to make a visit to the excellent National Wildflower Centre (NWFC), which is only 0.5 miles from the TPT NCN 62. To find the NWFC, cycle on from Sainsbury's at Knotty Ash for 0.7 miles and leave the TPT NCN 62 immediately after it goes under the M62. Take the A5080 Bowring Park Road for 0.5 miles to reach Court Hey Park and the entrance to the NWFC (**SJ 419 902**).

Otherwise, continue onwards from Sainsbury's following the TPT NCN 62 signposts to reach the A561 Speke Boulevard (**SJ 440 838**), which is 26.2 miles from the start at the Seamark. At this point turn left and continue to follow the NCN 62 signs. Cycle along South Road for 0.5 miles and then turn right going under the A561 Speke Boulevard via an underpass (**SJ 446 837**) (look out for broken glass). From the underpass turn left and cycle for 1.1 miles along Alderfield Drive, passing St Ambrose Roman Catholic Primary School to reach Hale Road (**SJ 450 826**). At this junction turn left and cycle for 1 mile to reach the High Street, Hale, and turn right. Continue on for a further 0.2 miles and you will arrive at the Childe of Hale public house (**SJ 469 822**) (6 Church End, Hale Village, Liverpool L24 4AX, tel. 0151 425 2954). The pub serves food between

Stage 1: Southport to Lymm

noon and 8pm each day and between noon and 7pm on Sundays. The Childe of Hale is 29 miles from the start at the Seamark in Southport.

If you have stopped for a drink or snack at the Childe of Hale you will have noticed the distinctive sandstone war memorial close to the pub at the junction of the High Street, Church End and Town Lane. To continue along the TPT keep the war memorial behind you and cycle out of Hale village along Town Lane and then into Hale Gate Road and, after 1 mile from the pub, turn right. A sign for United Utilities Wastewater Treatment identifies the turning. This junction (**SJ 480 833**) is 30 miles from the start at the Seamark and marks the start of a stretch of some tremendously enjoyable cycling as the TPT encroaches on

Stage 1: Southport to Lymm

The cycle-friendly entrance to the National Wildflower Centre.
(Photo: National Wildflower Centre)

the banks of the River Mersey with views of Widnes and Runcorn ahead. This section of the TPT passes through the award-winning Pickerings Pasture Nature Reserve (**SJ 489 835**).

Cycle through Pickerings Pasture and follow the TPT to reach a bridge over Ditton Brook where you will find a set of steep steps (**SJ 496 839**). Negotiate the steps and continue onwards for 1 mile to reach the unmistakeable Runcorn Widnes Bridge (**SJ 510 837**).

Cycle under the bridge and continue on the NCN 62. You will pass the Mersey public house and you should continue to head towards the river before turning left and following the NCN 62. Look out for a sign indicating Spike Island and the NCN 62 and follow the direction indicated. After 32.8 miles from the start point at the Seamark you will have reached Spike Island (**SJ 515 846**), and away in the distance you will see the eight 114-metre cooling towers and the single 200-metre chimney of the 2,000 megawatt Fiddler's Ferry Power Station.

Stage 1: Southport to Lymm

The distinctive war memorial at Hale.

Should you wish to spend a little time exploring this part of Widnes we highly recommend a visit to the nearby Catalyst Centre (**SJ 513 843**). This is an interactive museum devoted to chemistry and the important role that it plays in our everyday lives. The Catalyst Centre is situated next to the TPT. The museum is open Tuesday to Sunday from 10am to 5pm and admission (2013) for adults is £4.95. There is also a café within the museum.

From the distinctive Catalyst Centre, you should then cycle along the towpath of the disused St Helens Canal for 3.6 miles to reach the Ferry Tavern (**SJ 564 867**). Arriving at the pub marks 36.4 miles of the adventure. At this stage in the journey you will also need to change maps to Ordnance Survey Sheet 109: Manchester. The pub is open everyday from noon, with fish and chips being a speciality on Saturday and Sunday lunchtimes. From the Ferry Tavern cycle onwards, continuing to follow the TPT and NCN 62 signs. After approximately

Stage 1: Southport to Lymm

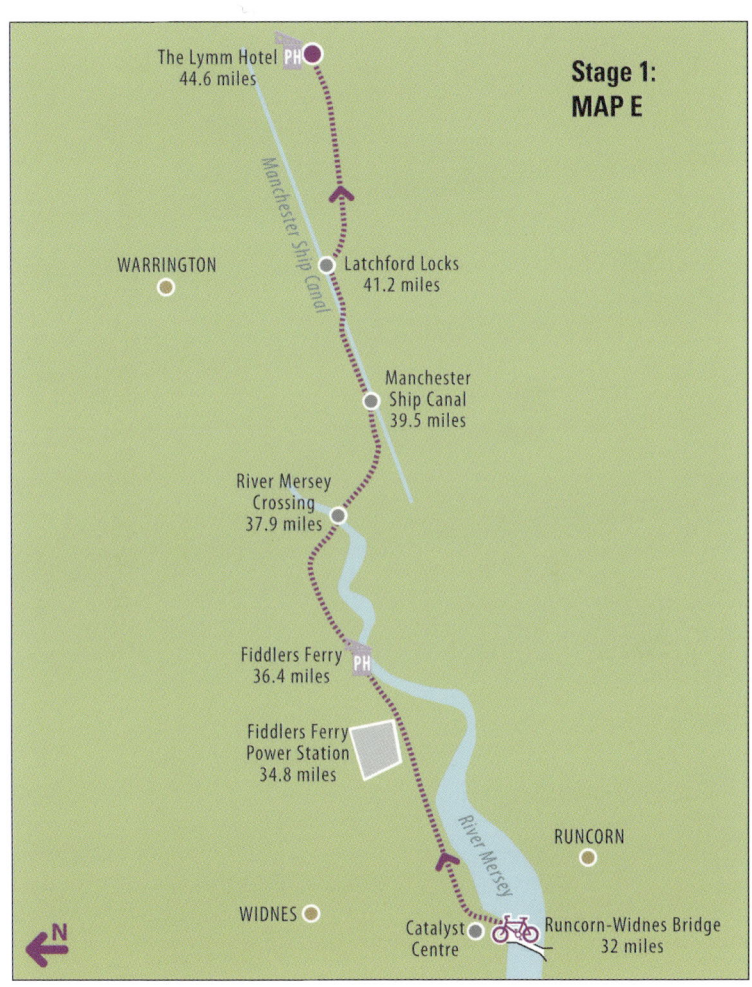

1.8 miles from the Ferry Tavern you will pass Gatewarth Community Recycling Centre, after which you will then cycle through the very peaceful Life For A Life Memorial Forest. Continue onwards for 1.2 miles to reach the A5060 Chester Road; turn left at the main road and continue for 0.1 miles to reach a distinctive

Stage 1: Southport to Lymm

Pickerings Pasture Nature Reserve on the banks of the River Mersey.

blue bridge (**SJ 603 864**). At the blue bridge turn right and continue along the TPT NCN 62. You will now have cycled 39.4 miles from the start at the Seamark in Southport.

As ever, you should continue following the TPT signs. The trail now goes off-road for 0.4 miles and you will pass Walton Lock before reaching Greenall's Avenue at its junction with Wilderspool Crescent: take care at the junction. At Wilderspool Crescent you should turn right and cycle along Greenall's Avenue for 80 yards and then turn left adjacent to 128 Greenall's Avenue. The TPT then weaves around the rear of the houses in Greenall's Avenue and follows a traffic-free path alongside the Manchester Ship Canal for around 0.3 miles before emerging onto the A49 Wilderspool Causeway at the Northwich Road Swing Bridge over the Manchester Ship Canal. You should take care crossing the A49. Follow the TPT sign, which is opposite, and cycle straight on.

Stage 1: Southport to Lymm

The Runcorn Widnes Bridge.

The next mile of the journey is off-road and again alongside the Manchester Ship Canal, after which you will emerge at the junction with the A50 Knutsford Road (**SJ 628 870**). At this location you will also find MJ Cycles (752 Knutsford Road, Warrington, Cheshire WA4 1JS, tel. 01925 650100), which is very convenient if you require running repairs to your bicycle. At this stage of the journey you will have cycled approximately 41.1 miles from the Seamark, Southport.

Cross the A50 and turn left and then turn almost immediately right in front of a new housing development named Williams Wharf. Remain on the TPT NCN 62 for approximately 0.6 miles to reach the imposing architecture of Latchford Locks (**SJ 638 873**). At this point the TPT NCN 62 crosses the Manchester Ship Canal.

Stage 1: Southport to Lymm

The Catalyst Centre, Widnes.

Stage 1: Southport to Lymm

MANCHESTER SHIP CANAL

The Manchester Ship Canal is an engineering treasure from the Victorian era. Constructed over 120 years ago at a cost of approximately £15 million, the canal is 35½ miles long, linking Eastham on the Mersey Estuary with Manchester. Naturally divided into two sections, the first 21 miles are from Eastham to Latchford, which are to a degree tidal, while the second section of 14½ miles from Latchford to Manchester is controlled by locks which lift vessels to a height of 60 feet to correspond to Manchester's height above sea level.

The canal was born out of the trading situation in Manchester in the second half of the nineteenth century. At that time the majority of Manchester's exports had to pass through Liverpool, where the railway companies and the Liverpool Dock Board exacted punitive charges on

Ship negotiating Latchford Locks in 1950. (Photo: Wikimedia Commons)

Stage 1: Southport to Lymm

Latchford Locks, looking east along the Manchester Ship Canal.

manufactured goods traded from Manchester. The city fathers were desperate to revitalize Manchester's economic fortunes and escape the control of their neighbours. At the end of June 1882 seventy merchants, bankers, financiers and manufacturers met at The Towers. This was the Didsbury home of engineer Daniel Adamson. These men agreed to form a provisional committee to construct the Manchester Ship Canal, which upon completion would effectively make Manchester an inland seaport. From this first meeting at Adamson's home it took eleven and a half years before the canal was filled with water and it eventually opened to vessels on 1 January 1894. These far-sighted Manchester businessmen were correct in their judgement. The canal did prove to be extremely effective in re-establishing the city's trade and export links across the world, which in turn brought renewed prosperity to the region.

Stage 1: Southport to Lymm

Having crossed the Manchester Ship canal at Latchford Locks, cycle for a very short distance to reach Thelwall New Road, turn left and then immediately right into Bradshaw Lane. Cycle along Bradshaw Lane for 150 yards and turn left onto a further off-road section of the TPT NCN 62. Cycle along this section of the TPT for 2.5 miles to reach the Ranger Centre (just off Statham Avenue, Lymm, Cheshire WA13 9NJ, tel. 01925 758195). The Ranger Centre is situated on a site once occupied by the former Lymm railway station. Close by, you will find the Macdonald Lymm Hotel (**SJ 679 875**), which is a very comfortable place in which to spend the night. The distance for today's stage of the ride is approximately 44.6 miles. If you are looking for a pleasant stroll in the evening, there is an interesting walk on the Lymm Heritage Trail, which takes in Lymm Dam and Lymm Slitting Mill.

STAGE 2:

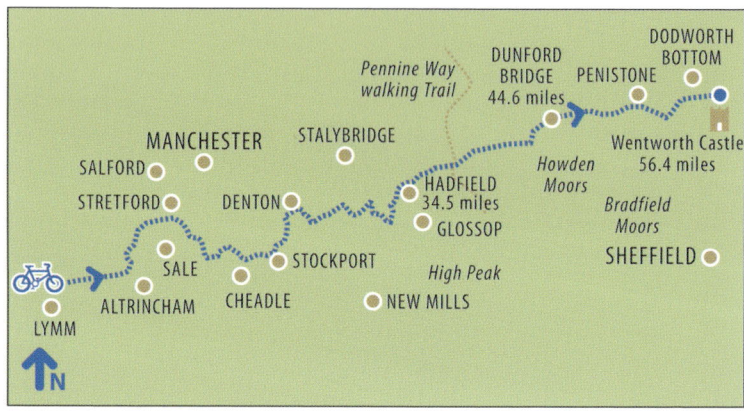

56.4 miles
Terrain: Hilly in parts

Maps required:
Ordnance Survey Landranger Sheet 109: Manchester
Ordnance Survey Landranger Sheet 110: Sheffield and Huddersfield

LYMM TO WENTWORTH CASTLE

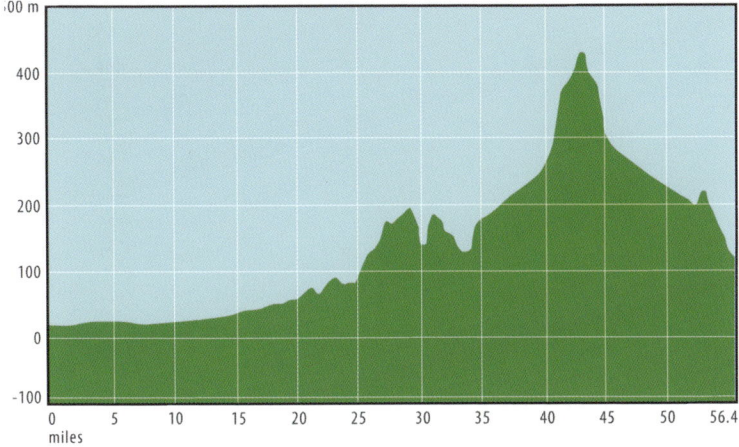

Having enjoyed a great day's cycling on the TPT through the urban landscape of Southport, Liverpool and Warrington, Stage 2 offers a little extra in terms of difficulty. The terrain is hilly east of Glossop and the navigation can be quite tricky through Stockport; however, the superb Peak District scenery and the views on offer of the South Pennines away to the north combined with the off-road nature of the TPT should make for another extremely enjoyable day in the saddle.

With the Ranger Centre, Lymm, as your start point, continue along the TPT for 1.4 miles to the junction with the A6144 Birch Brook Road (**SJ 698 882**). At this location you will find Cyclelife (1 Birchbrook Road, Lymm, Cheshire, WA13 9RR, tel. 01925 753424). This bicycle shop will undertake running repairs for riders completing the TPT. From Cyclelife continue for 75 yards to Chaise Meadow where you will find a Co-operative store, which is an opportune place to stock up with food. Cycle onwards on the NCN 62 along the trackbed of another former railway line, first opened in 1853 as part of the Warrington and Stockport Railway, to reach Seamon's Road (**SJ 751 889**). At this junction turn left and then immediately right into Dairyhouse Lane. This intersection is

Stage 2: Lymm to Wentworth Castle

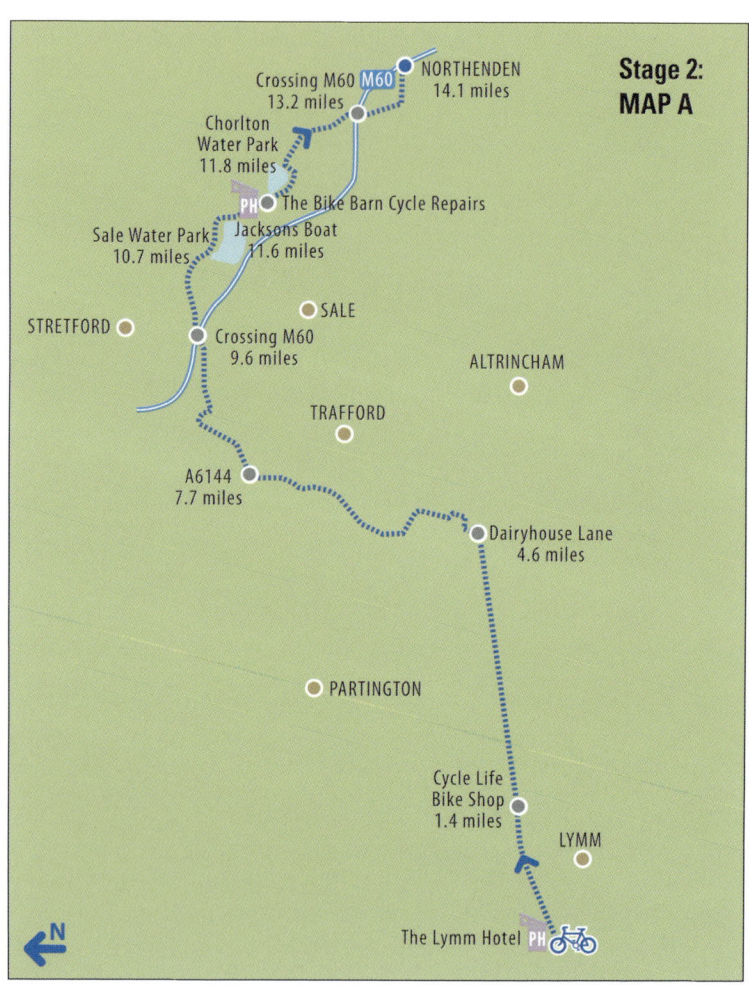

also signed for the TPT. You will have cycled approximately 4.6 miles from the Ranger Centre.

You should now cycle along Dairyhouse Lane for approximately 0.9 miles to reach the junction of Sinderland Road and turn left. Cycle on for 0.3 miles and turn right into Woodcote Road; this junction is clearly signed for the TPT. Follow

Stage 2: Lymm to Wentworth Castle

The TPT Ranger Service office at Lymm.

the signs for the TPT and you will cycle past Woodcote Equestrian Supplies and after approximately 0.9 miles from turning into Woodcote Road you will reach Ashton Road. You should now turn right and continue onwards for 1 mile to A6144 Carrington Lane at its junction with Banky Lane (**SJ 763 927**). This junction is 7.7 miles from the start of today's ride at the Ranger Centre, Lymm.

Cross the busy A6144 junction and bear right, cycling along the quieter Banky Lane, which runs parallel to the main road, and after approximately 0.9 miles re-cross the A6144 and follow the TPT NCN 62 as once again it follows an off-road course alongside the banks of the River Mersey. Cycle onwards for approximately 1 mile to a bridge which traverses the M60 (**SJ 785 936**); at this point you will have cycled approximately 9.6 miles from the Ranger Centre in Lymm.

The TPT NCN 62 now weaves around the A56 while heading towards Sale Water Park. After approximately 0.6 miles from the bridge over the M60 you will reach Hancock Street at its junction with Hawthorn Road

Stage 2: Lymm to Wentworth Castle

The River Mersey.

(**SJ 795 938**). At this point you should turn right, cycle through a bridge which goes under the Bridgewater Canal and then cycle past Stretford Cemetery (**SJ 798 938**) and continue onwards. At Hawthorn Road, Stretford, you will have completed approximately 10.2 miles from the start of today's journey at the Ranger Centre.

The next section of cycling is particularly enjoyable as the TPT NCN 62 traverses Sale Water Park and close to Broad Ees Dole Nature Reserve, the latter winning awards for creative conservation. In 2003 Broad Ees Dole was designated by Natural England to be of sufficient importance to award it Local Nature Reserve status, in line with the significant role its wetlands play for migratory birds and the variety of its plant life.

Continue onwards and follow the TPT NCN 62 as it again follows the banks of the River Mersey and into Chorlton Ees Nature Reserve. This nature reserve is noted as an excellent place for bird-watching: regulars often sight siskins, lesser redpolls, greenfinches and linnets in the trees and on the grassland, while other species such as reed buntings, whitethroats and blackcaps are known to breed here. The nature reserve was set up on reclaimed land from the old Withington sewage works.

Cycle away from Chorlton Ees Nature Reserve for 0.5 miles to reach Jackson's

Stage 2: Lymm to Wentworth Castle

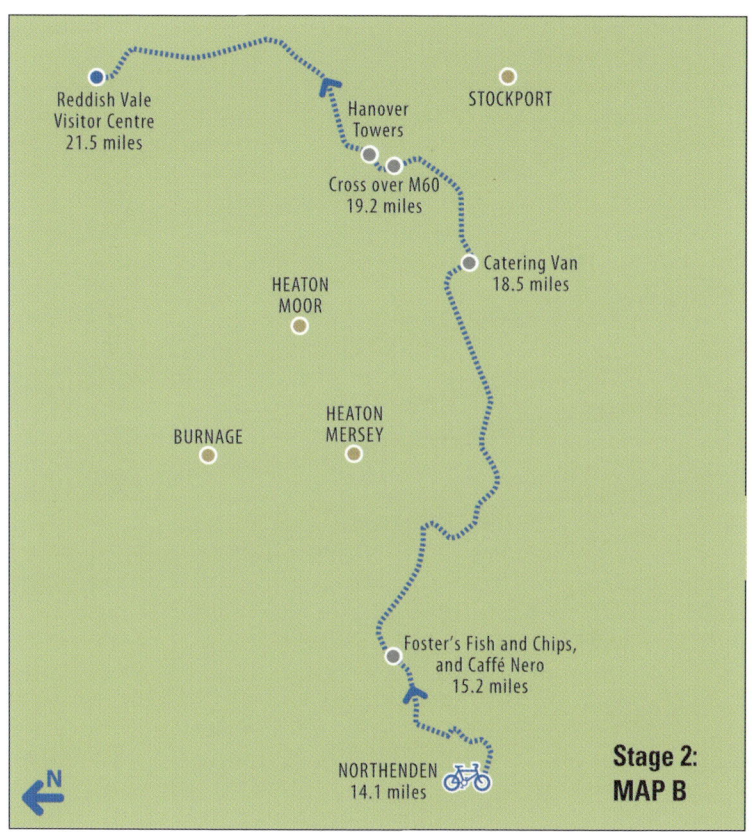

Boat (**SJ 811 926**), which is a historic pub on the south bank of the River Mersey. This is a great place to stop for a drink and it has a cycle repair facility due to its close business association with the nearby Bike Barn. Jackson's Boat is 11.6 miles into today's journey.

The off-road cycling along the banks of the River Mersey continues with the TPT well signposted as it heads eastward, and you should now be heading for Chorlton Water Park. Keep cycling with the River Mersey to your right and after 0.5 miles you will reach Chorlton Water Park. This is a 7.9-hectare manmade reservoir that is scientifically important because of its winter wildfowl

Stage 2: Lymm to Wentworth Castle

populations. It also forms part of the Mersey Valley Project, who administer and manage a number of countryside sites close to the River Mersey. Upon reaching Chorlton Water Park cycle around the lake and continue to follow the TPT NCN 62 as it follows an off-road course, avoiding major roads, to reach the village of Northenden. After 13.9 miles from the start at the Lymm Ranger Centre you should reach the Crown public house, Northenden (**SJ 832 901**), where you should turn left into Ford Lane.

Cycle past St Wilfrid's Church (**SJ 833 901**) and continue onwards on the TPT NCN 62; after 0.2 miles you will cycle under the M60. Remain on Ford Lane and go past the entrance to Didsbury Golf Club and after around 1 mile from cycling under the M60 at Northenden you will reach the junction of Ford Lane and Dene Road. Turn right and cycle for a mere 40 yards to reach the junction of Dene Road and A5145 Wilmslow Road. At this junction you will find Viceroy Court apartments in front of you and Fosters Fish and Chips (**SJ 846 908**) on the corner of Dene Road and Wilmslow Road. We highly recommend stopping at Fosters for lunch. At this junction you will have cycled 15.2 miles from the Ranger Centre, Lymm.

The next stage of the TPT features urban cycling and the most challenging navigation of the entire ride as you cycle from Didsbury to Stockport and beyond. At the time of cycling the reconnaissance ride in April 2012 there were temporary diversions to the TPT in place. The route described follows the TPT as it stood at this time. With Viceroy Court in front of you turn left onto the A5145 Wilmslow Road and cycle for approximately 100 yards; turn right at Caffè Nero (761–65 Wilmslow Road, Manchester, M20 6RN, tel. 0161 448 1343) (**SJ 847 909**) and cycle into Grange Lane. You should then cycle down Grange Lane to the junction and turn left into William Street. Cycle past the Fletcher Moss public house and turn right (**SJ 847 912**) into School Lane. Cycle along School Lane for approximately 0.6 miles to reach the A34 Kingsway and continue straight over this busy junction (**SJ 857 909**) into Queensway. Continue along Queensway for 0.1 miles and turn right into Burnage Lane (**SJ 858 908**). Continue along Burnage Lane for 0.2 miles to reach the junction with the A5145 Didsbury Road and turn left (**SJ 858 905**). The junction of the A5145 Didsbury Road and Burnage Lane is 16.4 miles from the start of your journey at the Ranger Centre, Lymm.

From the junction cycle along Didsbury Road for 0.3 miles and turn right into Station Road (**SJ 864 904**). Cycle down Station Road and bear right into Vale Road. After 0.5 miles from leaving the junction of the A5145 Didsbury Road and Station Road you will reach the offices of Delta Legal. Turn left at these offices and follow the TPT along the banks of the River Mersey for 1.2 miles

Stage 2: Lymm to Wentworth Castle

into Stockport. You will emerge from this off-road section of the TPT to rejoin the A5145 Didsbury Road. Cycle along Didsbury Road for a short distance and look out for the distinctive pyramid shape of the Co-operative Financial Services building away to your right. Continue on to the nearby Junction 1 of the M60 motorway, follow the TPT NCN 62 as it traverses the roundabout traffic-free to Hollywood Way (**SJ 884 901**) and then cycle into Yew Street. At this location you should find a mobile catering van which serves tea, coffee and excellent bacon rolls.

Cycle on from the catering van, re-cross the River Mersey and then turn left (**SJ 885 900**) onto the A560 Brinksway. Cycle on for approximately 0.5 miles along the A560 Brinksway into Chestergate and then just short of the huge railway bridge turn right (**SJ 891 902**) into Viaduct Street, where you should continue on for a further 120 yards and turn left into Wood Street, Stockport (**SJ 891 900**). Fortunately, the TPT NCN 62 is very well signed at this stage of the ride.

Continue along Wood Street for 0.1 miles to reach the junction with the busy A6 Wellington Street (**SJ 893 902**) and go straight over. For the next 0.4 miles you will be cycling through the very heart of Stockport town centre and following the numerous signposts for the TPT NCN 62. The route takes in Chestergate, Prince's Street and Tiviot Dale before reaching the noisy junction of A560 Knightsbridge, which is very close to the M60 motorway (**SJ 895 908**). This location marks approximately 19.2 miles of cycling from the start point at the Ranger Centre, Lymm. Take care crossing the A560 and then cycle along the B6167 Lancashire Hill for approximately 0.1 miles before turning right into Penny Lane (**SJ 895 909**). Cycle along this road for approximately 350 yards. You will pass a derelict public house on the left and the monolithic 1960s high-rise Hanover Towers in front of you.

At this point turn right and follow the now familiar TPT NCN 62 signs. After the traffic associated with traversing Stockport, it is now time for a period of calm and relaxing cycling. Continue for a further 0.5 miles to reach the A626 Tiviot Way (**SJ 900 914**). Cross over this busy road and continue onwards (off-road) for 1.7 miles to reach Reddish Vale Visitor Centre (**SJ 904 935**). This short section of the ride is lovely as the TPT NCN 62 wends its way close to the River Tame and through woodland rich in wildlife to arrive at the Visitor Centre. You will now have cycled approximately 21.5 miles from the Ranger Centre in Lymm. It may be worth stopping for a short break and speaking with one of the wardens at the Visitor Centre. These dedicated volunteers have a wealth of knowledge regarding the natural history of the area. In addition you may encounter someone working at the centre who is very familiar with the

Stage 2: Lymm to Wentworth Castle

Hanover Towers in Stockport, a highly visible navigational waypoint.

Stage 2: Lymm to Wentworth Castle

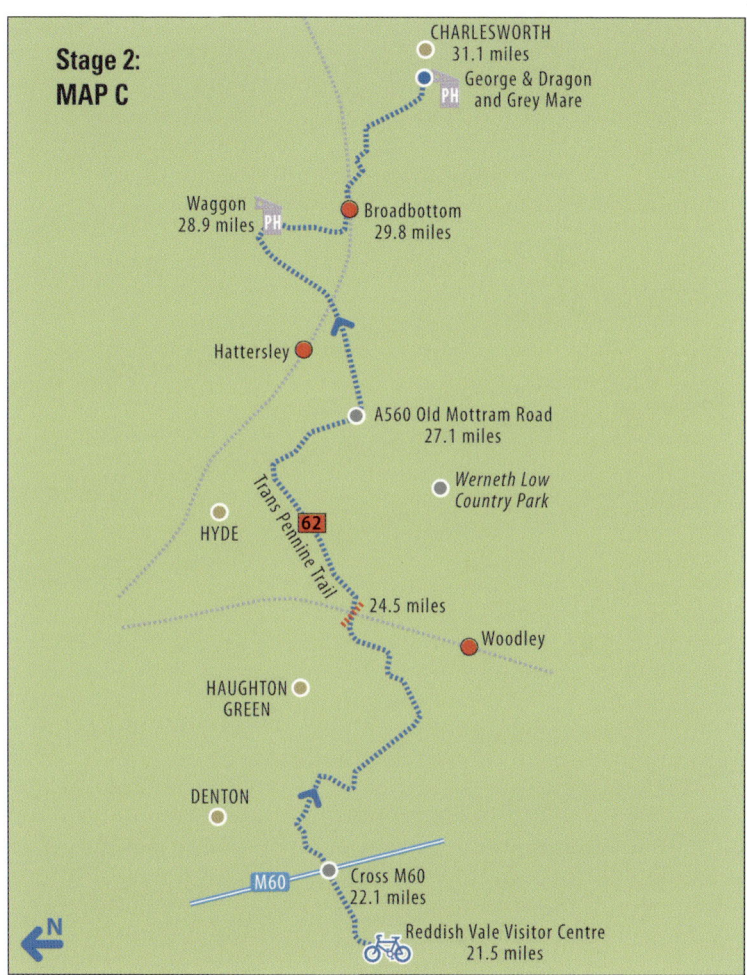

industrial history of Reddish Vale and able to explain in detail how in the 1860s it was once home to a thriving calico print works.

After a suitable break you should be ready to resume for a couple of hours of more challenging cycling. Depart from the Reddish Vale Visitor Centre and continue along the TPT NCN 62. After approximately 0.6 miles you will cross

Stage 2: Lymm to Wentworth Castle

the M60 (**SJ 913 940**). Cycle onwards for a further 0.4 miles to reach the junction with Kingsley Close and turn right. Continue along Kingsley Close and after 0.1 miles turn right into a rather concealed turning next to 19 Kingsley Close. This turning is signposted for the TPT. Cycle along this stretch of cycle path for a further 0.1 mile to rejoin the road at Mill Lane and then cycle along Yew Tree Road for 0.2 miles to reach the junction with the A6017 Stockport Road, Denton (**SJ 923 942**). You will now have cycled 23 miles from the start point at the Ranger Station.

Cycle down the A6017 Stockport Road for 0.3 miles and turn left (**SJ 922 937**); this turning is clearly signed for the TPT, Broadbottom 8 miles. Once again you will be able to enjoy a 3.8-mile section of tremendous cycling as the TPT NCN 62 follows an off-road path through Haughton Dale (**SJ 936 930**). The TPT then runs along the trackbed of another former railway line first operated by the Manchester, Sheffield and Lincolnshire Railway. You should follow the TPT through Hyde before turning off onto Green Lane (**SJ 961 946**), where the route ascends along the very rough surface of Green Lane while going past Godley Stud Riding School to reach the A560 Mottram Old Road (**SJ 965 937**). At this stage of your journey you will have cycled approximately 27.1 miles from the start point at the Ranger Centre.

At the junction of the A560 Mottram Old Road turn left and cycle onwards for approximately 1.3 miles. You should go past the Chapman Arms public house before taking the next right turn into Clough End Road (**SJ 985 947**). From here cycle on for 65 yards and turn left into Broadbent Grove and continue for 0.2 miles to the end of the road before turning right into Chair Bar Lane. You should now continue for a further 0.1 miles, turn right and cycle off-road. Follow this cycle path for approximately 0.2 miles and you will emerge onto Broadbottom Road with the Waggon public house (175 Broadbottom Road, Mottram in Longdendale, Hyde, SK14 6HY, tel. 01457 763 787) immediately in front of you (**SJ 989 946**). The pub does serve meals although it is worth ringing ahead for further details. At this stage of the journey you will have travelled 28.9 miles from the start point at the Ranger Centre.

With the Waggon pub in front of you, turn right and continue to cycle onwards. You will then pass Broadbottom railway station (**SJ 990 938**) and after 1 mile you will cross the River Etherow. At this point follow the TPT sign for Longdendale, and you will need to change to Ordnance Survey Sheet 110: Sheffield and Huddersfield. From crossing the River Etherow continue along Long Lane for 0.9 miles to reach the junction of Long Lane and the A626 Glossop Road at Charlesworth (**SK 005 929**) and turn left. You will now have completed approximately 30.8 miles of your journey from the Ranger Centre.

Stage 2: Lymm to Wentworth Castle

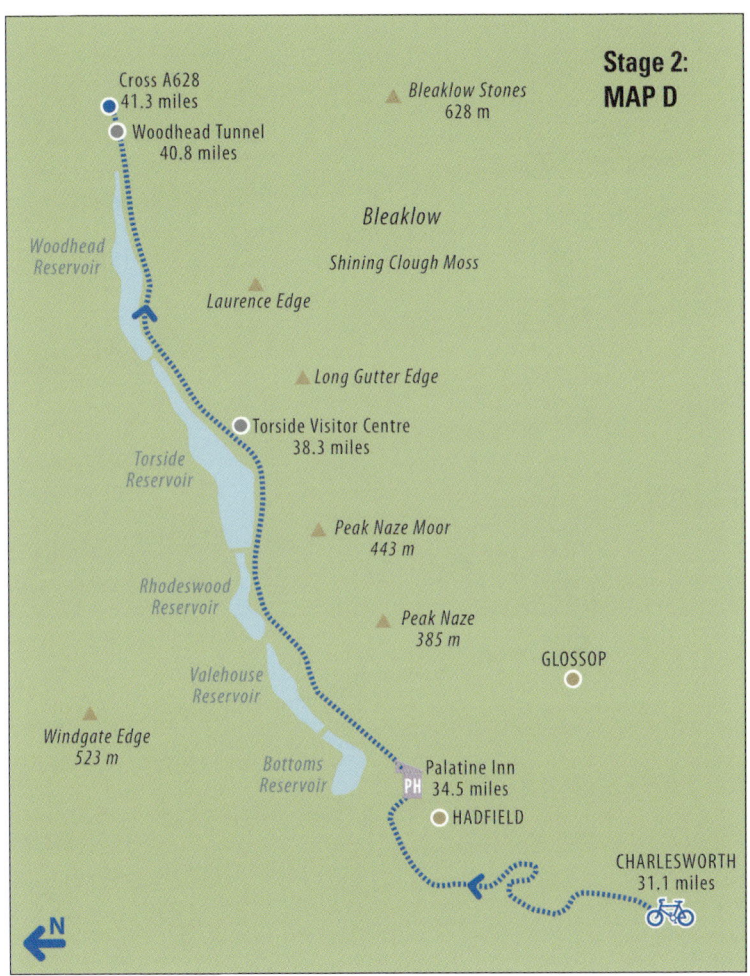

There are two pubs in Charlesworth: the Grey Mare (01457 853 828) and the George and Dragon (01457 860 123). Neither pub has a website and due to the economic climate both pubs frequently change opening hours to suit demand. It is worth phoning ahead to ensure that they are not closed.

Having turned left at the junction of Long Lane and Glossop Road, cycle

Stage 2: Lymm to Wentworth Castle

Plaque marking the site of Melandra Roman Fort.

onwards for 0.7 miles and turn left (**SK 009 941**) following the TPT signs. As you cycle through a suburban housing estate you will pass the site of Melandra Roman Fort (**SK 010 952**).

Continue to follow the TPT signs and descend to cross the River Etherow before reaching the pedestrian crossing at the A57 Woolley Bridge (**SK 010 955**). Cross the A57 and again follow the TPT signs. At this stage of the journey you will have cycled 33.2 miles from the start point at the Ranger Centre. Cycle onwards following the off-road TPT for 0.3 miles to reach Woolley Bridge Road and turn right (**SK 011 959**), once again following signs for the TPT NCN 62 and Longdendale. After a further 120 yards you will pass the Pear Tree Inn public house. Remain on Woolley Bridge Road following signs for the TPT Longdendale. From this junction (the Pear Tree pub) cycle on for 0.6 miles and at the junction of Woolley Bridge Road, Bankbottom and Station Road (**SK 020 965**) you will see a blue TPT NCN 62/68 sign indicating left to Longdendale, Tintwistle and Hadfield Industrial Estate, and a brown tourist information sign indicating right

Stage 2: Lymm to Wentworth Castle

to the Longdendale Trail. Do not turn left, *turn right* and cycle up the hill and into Station Road.

There is an excellent fish and chip shop here, Billy's Plaice (98–102 Station Road, Hadfield, SK13 1AJ, open Monday to Saturday 11.30am to 2pm, tel. 01457 868045). Continue up the hill and at the top of Station Road, Hadfield, opposite Hadfield railway station, you will find the Palatine Inn (tel. 01457 852 459) (**SK 023 961**), a handy place for a drink before tackling the Longdendale Trail. The popular BBC series *The League of Gentlemen* was filmed in and around Hadfield.

From the Palatine Inn (look out for the distinctive war memorial opposite), bear left and cycle into Platt Street and after a mere 0.1 miles join the off-road section of the TPT which begins in the car park in Platt Street (**SK 025 962**). You will have cycled approximately 34.5 miles from the start point at the Ranger Centre.

THE LONGDENDALE VALLEY

The TPT designers did a sterling service when they chose the 170-year-old trackbed of the former Sheffield, Ashton-under-Lyne and Manchester Railway to become part of the TPT route. Running from Hadfield to Woodhead it is known as the Longdendale Trail. This is a splendid part of the journey enhanced by spectacular landscape and packed full of natural and engineering history. The trail lies within the Dark Peak, a section of the Peak District National Park at the southern edge of the Pennine hills. The Dark Peak is renowned for its moorland with the underlying rocks consisting of brown sandstone, shales and darker millstone grit that combine with differing shades of dun and tawny heather to give the landscape its distinctive identity. Cycling away from Hadfield you will see towering escarpments such as Peak Naze, Long Gutter Edge, Bradwell Sitch, Deer Knowl and Dowstone Rocks, whilst on the plateau beyond lies Bleaklow at 630 metres above sea level. Piercing these escarpments are steep gullies known as cloughs, which are banked with verdant foliage and carry water from the moorland plateau. After periods of heavy rain the cloughs cascade with water from the hills to the reservoirs below.

On the valley floor at Longdendale there are five reservoirs that are collectively known as the Longdendale Chain, and they inject a steely grey-coloured base to the surrounding landscape. The first reservoir you will encounter en route to the Woodhead Tunnel is Bottoms; as you progress further east you will pass Valehouse, Rhodeswood, Torside and finally Woodhead. The reservoirs

Stage 2: Lymm to Wentworth Castle

were constructed in Victorian times to supply the population of Manchester with clean drinking water. John Frederick Bateman led the construction project. He was an exceptional water engineer who had spent time studying the geographical features of the Longdendale valley and came to recognize how its high annual rainfall would make it an ideal location for a chain of reservoirs to supply water to the nearby villages and towns of Derbyshire and the expanding city of Manchester.

Construction work began on the Longdendale Chain in August 1848, when 1,000 labourers, stonemasons and miners descended on the valley to begin work on the Woodhead Reservoir, the first to be slated for construction as part of this ambitious project. Over the next three decades workers braved the elements in this inhospitable part of the Pennines using horses, steam power and sheer physical strength to build what would become, for a time at least, the largest chain of reservoirs in the world. A year after work on Woodhead Reservoir commenced, engineering began on both Rhodeswood and Torside Reservoirs and in July 1865 construction began on Valehouse Reservoir. The final phase of the project began in November 1867 and, with the exception of Woodhead, the reservoirs took an average of almost nine years to build. Woodhead Reservoir proved exceptionally difficult and the engineers struggled for years to make it watertight; it eventually took twenty-nine years to complete. Despite the delays with Woodhead Reservoir, by 1855 work was sufficiently advanced for freshwater to begin flowing from the Longdendale valley towards Manchester. The outstanding Bateman, his engineering colleagues and the indomitable labourers had triumphed and today they would be proud to know that their reservoirs have never run dry. Every day the Longdendale Chain supplies around 22.5 million gallons of water to the people of Glossop, Tameside, Stockport and east Manchester.

There are a number of conveniently sited benches on the ride through the Longdendale valley toward the Woodhead Tunnel. These provide a very peaceful place to sit and enjoy the copious bird life of the area. A rare species you may come across between late March and September is the ring ouzel, which winters in southern Spain and the Atlas Mountain regions of Morocco and Algeria.

The ring ouzel is known locally as the 'moor blackbird' and is most likely to be sighted close to one of the many cloughs at the side of the trail. Pause and listen for the distinctive tac-tac-tac sound of its voice. The ring ouzel is easily identifiable; as its nickname suggests it looks very similar to a blackbird although a little smaller and slimmer. The male has sooty black plumage with a distinctive white crescent. It will perch on rocks or bushes and eat worms, insects and fruit such as raspberries, blackberries and cherries.

Stage 2: Lymm to Wentworth Castle

Woodhead Reservoir.

Ring ouzel. (Photo: Tim Melling)

Stage 2: Lymm to Wentworth Castle

Whinchat. (Photo: Wikimedia Commons)

From spring to late summer you may also sight a whinchat, identifiable by a white stripe above its eye. It has streaky brown upperparts and a light-orange coloured breast. The whinchat moves along the ground in rapid hops and bobs while flicking its tail and wings. It will rest on the tops of bushes or large ground plants and flies low as it moves from one perch to the other with a jerky style of flight while rapidly moving its wings.

You should also look out for the wheatear; this is a small, short-tailed, dainty bird which is the size of a sparrow. The wheatear winters in southern and central Africa and is a summer visitor to the upland areas of northern Britain such as Longdendale. It is active and restless, flying short distances in a succession of hops, and perches on walls, fences and posts.

The meadow pipit is the dominant breeding species of the Peak District moorland and is around 5 inches long. This gregarious bird can be sighted hopping along the ground and flying in short bursts. It has brownish grey

Stage 2: Lymm to Wentworth Castle

Wheatear. (Photo: Wikimedia Commons)

plumage and in summer you should expect to see it in the pastures very close to the cycle path.

One bird you are almost guaranteed to see close to the cycle path is the red grouse. This is a reddish-brown game bird common to the Longdendale valley. The red grouse is a resident of the upland moors, low-lying mosses and boggy areas. The first indication of this bird is usually a commotion caused by the sound of breaking heather and a cackling cry of 'bak, bak, ak, ak' as it appears rapidly beating its wings, while flying and gliding for distances of up to half a mile away from perceived danger.

Stage 2: Lymm to Wentworth Castle

Meadow pipit. (Photo: G. Zambonini)

WOODHEAD TUNNEL

After a steady ride of some 40.8 miles from the Ranger Centre at Lymm you will eventually reach the Woodhead Tunnel (**SK 114 998**). Rather confusingly there are in fact three tunnels at Woodhead. The largest tunnel was constructed after the Second World War and is usually referred to as the British Rail (BR) tunnel. The two smaller tunnels are from the Victorian era. The tunnel in the centre (of the three) was the first to be built and is known as the down-road, while the tunnel furthest to the left is known as the up-road.

The history of the construction of the tunnels at Woodhead is absorbing. In 1836 the extent of the rail network in Britain amounted to a mere 300 miles – although this was about to change as entrepreneurs and industrialists scrambled to construct more lines and take advantage of the commercial opportunities presented by the Industrial Revolution. The merchants and manufacturers of Sheffield were particularly keen to exploit the trading opportunities that rail communication with Manchester and Liverpool would bring.

Stage 2: Lymm to Wentworth Castle

The tunnels at Woodhead as they look today.

Woodhead Station, 1910. (Photo: J. Quick)

Stage 2: Lymm to Wentworth Castle

The fledgling Sheffield, Ashton-under-Lyne and Manchester Railway was launched on 4 January 1837, when a committee formed to raise £800,000 to build a railway across the Pennines. As with many new railway companies, raising the capital for the scheme proved problematic. Despite some financial difficulties, Lord Wharncliffe, the first chairman of the new company, broke the ground to signal the start of the project at a slate quarry halfway between Saltersbrook and Woodhead.

Preliminary work to drive the tunnel commenced immediately with vertical shafts being drilled into the hillside at Woodhead, although it was not until September 1839 that work on the tunnel began in earnest. To the west of the tunnel towards Manchester the more straightforward task of laying the track was forging ahead, with the new railway line being opened in sections. The first section opened in November 1841, running between Travis Street, Manchester and Godley Toll Bar. The new track was gradually being extended and by 24 December 1842 it was running as far as Dinting (close to Glossop); by the summer of 1844 it had reached Woodhead. A year later the stretch to the east from Dunford Bridge to Sheffield was also complete.

The remaining task was to finish the tunnel at Woodhead and from the very beginning of the project the engineers had a formidable job on their hands. Before excavation of the tunnel could even begin it was necessary to build 4 miles of tracks over the barren moorland to allow for the movement of materials and spoil to and from the tunnel bore. In addition, the contractors had to house hundreds of labourers or 'navvies' as they were known close to the construction site. They did this by erecting the most rudimentary accommodation for the labourers. They also built stables, gunpowder magazines and workshops, which in itself took nearly a year.

The conditions for the tunnel 'navvies' were appalling. They had to live close to the tunnel entrance and when at work they were to be found 500 feet underground digging and blasting their way through millstone grit, shale, sandstone and clay. Excavation was usually carried out by hand although a dangerous practice called 'knocking the legs out' was also used. This was essentially cutting and blasting the rock so that it fell vertically. This caused numerous casualties amongst the 'navvies'. It was not unusual for the men to work long hours, seven days a week, toiling knee-deep in mud, often slaking their thirst with the foul water that dripped down the walls of their subterranean workplace.

In addition to the horrendous living conditions and the back-breaking and dangerous nature of the work, the men were further exploited by the 'tommy shop' system whereby the sale of provisions was let out to a contractor who, because of the isolated nature of the construction site, charged a premium for

Stage 2: Lymm to Wentworth Castle

the goods. These dreadful conditions were noted in June 1845 when Dr John Roberton, a Manchester surgeon, visited the site. His findings were subsequently reported to Parliament. Roberton reported that there had been thirty-two fatal accidents and an incredible number of other injuries, including compound fractures, burns, cuts, part amputations and dislocations. There were no medical facilities at the tunnel and the only medical cover was provided by a local doctor who would visit and treat the injured. This welfare visit was funded by the men themselves, who contributed a small amount each week to pay for the doctor's services.

Despite the brutal working conditions the energy, determination and fortitude of the construction workers prevailed and the tunnel was finally opened on 22 December 1845. The following day the Sheffield, Ashton and Manchester Railway commenced operations, providing the first ever rail link between Manchester and Sheffield. At 3 miles 22 yards, the Woodhead Tunnel was the longest in the country. It had taken six years to build, cost £200,000, while exacting a far greater price in terms of lives lost and health ruined.

Only two years after opening, the down-road tunnel was operating at full capacity and it was apparent that a second bore was needed. Construction began on the new up-road in 1847 and by 2 February 1852 it had been completed, although once again it was not achieved without loss of life. In 1849 the workers' camp was ravaged by a cholera epidemic which claimed twenty-eight lives. As soon as the second tunnel, the up-road, was open, the down-road was closed to enable essential maintenance, and once this was dealt with both the up-road and down-road tunnels operated for almost a century.

The tunnels suffered from the consistent pounding of up to eighty steam trains a day and the backlog of repairs from the Second World War coalesced to place enormous strain on the fabric of both the up-road and down-road tunnels. Almost a century after construction the two tunnels were almost beyond repair, necessitating the construction of a third Woodhead tunnel. The contract for the work was awarded to Messrs Balfour Beatty and Company and work commenced in February 1949. This time there were decent facilities for the workers with a makeshift camp constructed in nearby Dunford Bridge, although tragically six workers died during this latest phase of construction. The pilot bore for the BR tunnel was finished on 16 May 1951 and by October 1953 the tunnel itself had been completed at a cost of £4.5 million.

The BR tunnel was 3 miles 66 yards long and equipped for electric locomotives. It was formally opened on 3 June 1954 by the Rt Hon. Alan Lennox-Boyd PC MP, the Minister of Transport and Civil Aviation. Once again, labourers and engineers at Woodhead had shown their mettle by constructing a new tunnel

Stage 2: Lymm to Wentworth Castle

in exceptionally difficult conditions. From now on, Sheffield and Manchester would be connected by the most modern electrified railway line in the country.

In the ensuing years following completion of the BR tunnel, rail transport at Woodhead passed without incident. This was until the early 1960s when the Central Electricity Generating Board (CEGB) put forward a proposal to run pylons from Dunford Bridge to Woodhead, as part of a new electricity supergrid stretching from Thorpe Marsh Power Station to Stalybridge, near Manchester. Various pressure groups raised objections to the project, forcing CEGB to look for alternative ways of running the supergrid over Woodhead. The old disused Victorian tunnels provided an almost tailor-made solution and, although the down-road tunnel was in a state of chronic disrepair and beyond use, work started in 1965 to renovate the up-road tunnel.

This in itself presented a significant challenge because massive soot deposits had built up inside the tunnel. Despite the difficulties the engineers pressed on and the work was eventually completed in October 1969 when the circuits were energized. With the down-road tunnel disused and the up-road tunnel carrying 400kV high voltage cabling, the third BR tunnel at Woodhead finally closed to passenger-carrying rail traffic on 5 November 1970. The line was not rendered completely unused because right through until the late 1970s trains passed through the BR tunnel carrying coal to Fiddler's Ferry Power Station to the west. This arrangement continued for over a decade before the BR tunnel closed forever on 17 July 1981. That almost brings the tale of engineering and transport at Woodhead to an end, except that the old Victorian up-road tunnel which has carried 400kV cabling for over forty years is now in a state of severe deterioration. The National Grid, the current owners, are about to close the up-road tunnel and install new high voltage electricity cabling into the BR tunnel, ending forever the possibility that trains may once again pass through the hillside at Woodhead.

We hope you will have enjoyed this snapshot of Victorian and post-war engineering. From the tunnels cycle on for a very short distance, turn left at a wooden signpost and then ascend to reach the very busy A628; take extra care at this point. Cross the road and then rejoin the off-road section of the TPT for a further 1.3 miles. You should re-cross the A628 (**SK 134 998**), again taking extra care, and then cycle along the off-road section of the TPT for 0.7 miles to reach Goddard Lane (**SE 141 005**) at its junction with the A628, near Gallows Moss.

Arriving at Gallows Moss marks one of the highest parts of the TPT, giving a spectacular perspective on the Yorkshire countryside. To the right you will see Windleden Reservoir and, beyond, Winscar Reservoir.

In this area you may be lucky enough to observe a short-eared owl. This bird has mottled tawny brown plumage, is active in the daytime and can be sighted

Stage 2: Lymm to Wentworth Castle

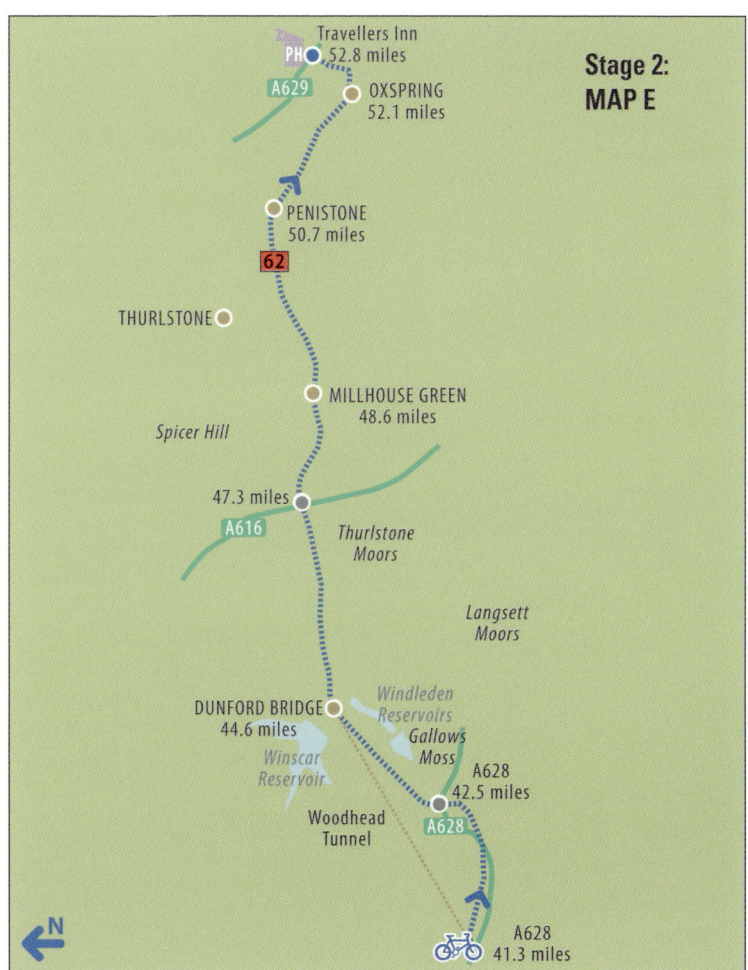

all year round on open moorland. It will settle on the ground or perch in trees, bushes or on fence-posts. The short-eared owl is identifiable by its long narrow wings and slow silent flight. Look out for it gliding and wheeling; when it is hunting it will fly over open areas only a few feet above the ground. Its favourite prey are short-tailed voles but they will take field mice, shrews, rats and young rabbits.

Stage 2: Lymm to Wentworth Castle

Short-eared owl. (Photo: Wikimedia Commons)

The kestrel is the bird of prey you are most likely to see on this section of moorland: a bird that can be sighted all year round and one that perches in trees and on fences. The kestrel flies with rapid wing beats, while its most distinctive feature is the way it hovers hanging in the air, head to wind, with its tail lowered. The kestrel will quickly fan its wings as it surveys the ground below for its quarry. If nothing is sighted it will move on for a few yards and repeat the process. Once the kestrel spots its prey it will make a fast angled descent for the kill. The kestrel will attack small birds as they feed on the ground or just as they are taking flight. It will also take field mice, moles, shrews and beetles.

One very rare bird you may be extremely fortunate to observe on Gallows

Stage 2: Lymm to Wentworth Castle

Kestrel. (Photo: Andreas Trepte) *Merlin. (Photo: Shay Connelly)*

Moss is the United Kingdom's smallest raptor, the merlin. This bird is not much bigger than a mistle thrush but its diminutive size should prevent misidentification. Look out for its rapid wing beats and dashing quick flight. It will glide, dip and swerve close to the ground. The merlin will perch on rocks, boulders, walls and fences. It relies on speed and agility when hunting, preferring to take its quarry in the air; it will fly low and fast, pursuing smaller birds such as meadow pipits, twites and skylarks.

The Longdendale Valley and the higher moorland nearby is also home to the mountain hare, a species that was introduced into the Peak District in the nineteenth century from Scotland to provide sport for wealthy local landowners.

Stage 2: Lymm to Wentworth Castle

Mountain hare. (Photo: J. Fielding)

The mountain hare is distinguished from the brown hare by its shorter ears and tail and is now well established in the Dark Peak area. They are active at dawn and dusk and during the daytime will often be found under the cover of rocks, boulders and clumps of heather. They moult three times a year and are very conspicuous in March and early April when the winter snow has melted and they are still to be found in their white winter coat.

From the spectacular plateau at Gallows Moss turn left and follow the signs for Dunford Bridge and the TPT. Cycle along Goddard Lane, then Windle Edge for 1.6 miles and then turn right just after the now-closed Stanhope Arms (**SE 158 023**) public house. You will then cycle into a large car park and rejoin the off-road section of the TPT towards Penistone. At this stage of the journey you will have cycled 44.6 miles from the start at the Ranger Centre, Lymm. The TPT NCN 62 once again takes a familiar off-road course along the trackbed of a former railway line and you should continue onwards for another 7.5 miles to reach the village of Oxspring, where you will be leaving the off-road section of the trail. For those who may be feeling a little tired, Penistone is a convenient place to stay for the evening.

Stage 2: Lymm to Wentworth Castle

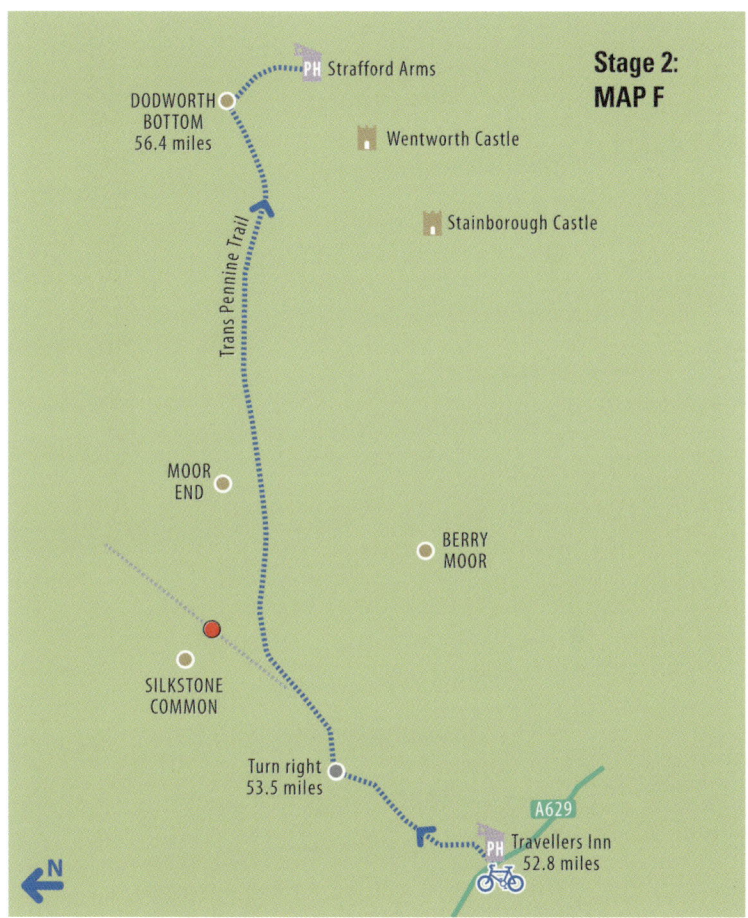

Having left the off-road section at Oxspring (**SE 265 023**), you should then turn left into Back Lane and cycle along The Willows for approximately 0.1 miles to reach the junction with Goddard Lane and then turn right. Cycle along the B6462 Goddard Lane for 0.3 miles to reach Roughbirchworth Lane (**SE 270 021**), where you should bear left and remain on this road for a further 0.2 miles to reach Bower Hill. Turn left (**SE 272 021**) at this junction

Stage 2: Lymm to Wentworth Castle

and cycle along Bower Hill for 0.5 miles to reach the Travellers Inn (Oxspring S36 8YJ, tel. 01226 762 518). The pub serves food on a daily basis although it is wise to ring ahead to check serving times. Having reached the Travellers Inn at the junction of the A629 Jockey Road and the B6449 Coates Lane (**SE 276 027**), you will have cycled approximately 52.8 miles from the start of the day's ride in Lymm.

Continue past the Travellers Inn, cycle along the B6449 Coates Lane for 0.1 miles before turning left into the charmingly named Maggot Lane (**SE 278 028**) and cycle for 0.6 miles before turning right (**SE 282 036**) and remaining on the TPT NCN 62. Once again you will be cycling off-road in the general direction of Barnsley. Continue on the off-road section of the TPT for approximately 2.7 miles to a convenient finish point which is marked by a distinctive battered and beaten sign for Wentworth Castle (**SE 323 044**). The conclusion of the day's ride from the Ranger Centre at Lymm to the turn-off for Wentworth Castle is approximately 56.4 miles.

All that remains is to travel to your accommodation in the nearby vicinity. We highly recommend Tankersley Manor Hotel, approximately 4.8 miles away; to reach the hotel you should leave the TPT NCN 62, turning right and following the signs for Wentworth Castle. Cycle down Smithy Wood Lane for 0.1 miles and join Gilroyd Lane, where you should cycle onwards for 0.2 miles to the junction of Round Green Lane, Lowe Lane and Park Drive. Ahead you will see the Strafford Arms (**SE 325 038**) (Park Drive, Stainborough, S75 3EW, tel. 01226 287 488), which is a handy place for a final drink.

The battered sign for Wentworth Castle signifies the conclusion of the day's stage.

Stage 2: Lymm to Wentworth Castle

To continue to the Tankersley Manor Hotel, turn left at the Strafford Arms junction and continue to cycle onwards along Round Green Lane and Rockley Lane for 2 miles (from leaving the TPT at the Wentworth Castle turn), at which point you will be cycling under the M1 (**SE 339 018**). Continue onwards for a further 0.9 miles to reach the A61 Sheffield Road (**SE 346 006**) and turn right, cycle along Sheffield Road for 0.2 miles, turn right into Moor Lane (**SE 349 004**) and cross the M1 via a traffic-free bridge (**SE 348 003**). Continue onwards for a short distance to reach New Road; turn left and cycle onwards, going under the A61 Westwood New Road (**SE 349 000**). Continue on for 0.1 miles to reach Tankersley Lane. Turn right (**SK 349 999**), cycle on for 0.2 miles to reach Church Lane (**SK 349 997**) and bear right and continue on for a final 0.5 miles to arrive at Tankersley Manor Hotel (**SK 343 994**).

STAGE 3:

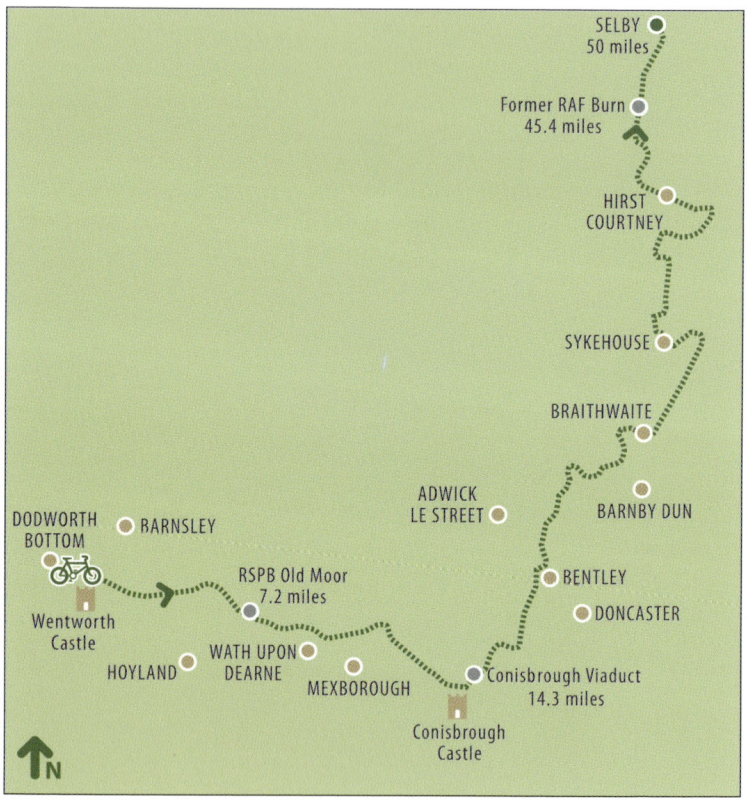

50 miles
Terrain: Flat

Maps required:
Ordnance Survey Landranger Sheet 110: Sheffield and Huddersfield
Ordnance Survey Landranger Sheet 111: Sheffield and Doncaster
Ordnance Survey Landranger Sheet 105: York and Selby

WENTWORTH CASTLE TO SELBY

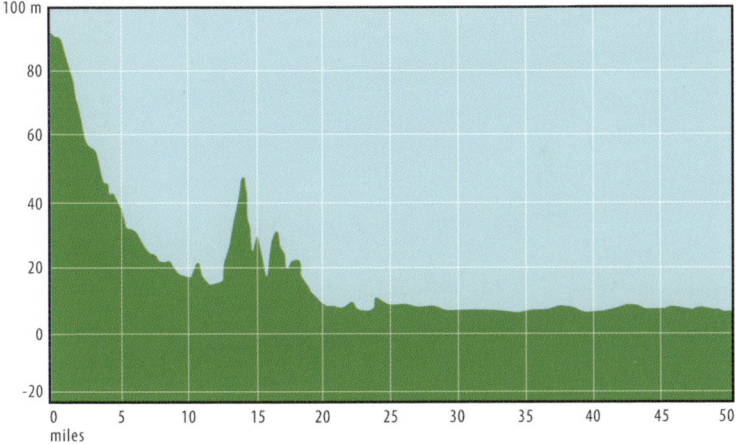

Today's start-point (yesterday's finish) is at the battered signpost on the TPT for Wentworth Castle (**SE 323 044**). After the now familiar photograph to mark the start of the day's ride, cycle along the off-road section of the TPT NCN 62 for 0.4 miles to cross the M1 (**SE 330 045**). Continue on from crossing the M1 for 1.1 miles to reach Wigfield Farm (**SE 345 037**), which is a satellite of Barnsley College. In a novel approach, the students are responsible for the day-to-day running of the farm assisted by conventionally employed staff. Although early in the day, you will find a café at Wigfield Farm, which is open daily between 10am and 4pm.

Away to the right, close to Wigfield Farm, you will see Worsbrough Reservoir and after 1.9 miles from the start-point you will cross the A61 at Park Road (**SE 352 036**). Continue along the off-road section of the TPT NCN 62. At this stage in the journey you will need to change to Ordnance Survey Sheet 111: Sheffield and Doncaster. Cycle onwards and after 7.2 miles from the start you will then reach RSPB Old Moor Nature Reserve (**SE 423 022**). This is a gorgeous place in which to take a well-earned breather, where you will be rewarded with a panorama of fields, skies and freshwater lakes.

Stage 3: Wentworth Castle to Selby

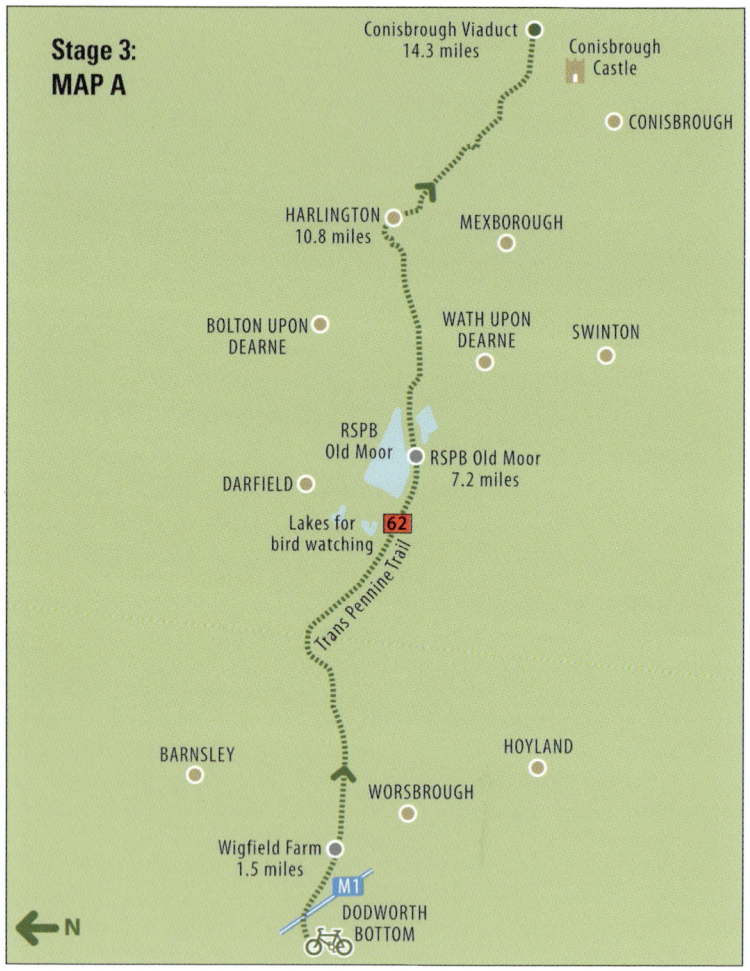

Stage 3: Wentworth Castle to Selby

DEARNE VALLEY RSPB OLD MOOR NATURE RESERVE

The TPT delivers a number of surprises, one of which is the traffic-free section of the trail from Worsbrough, which meanders into the Dearne Valley alongside lakes, damp grassland and copses. Around thirty years ago this part of the Dearne Valley looked totally different: it was the beating heart of the British coal mining industry. In the 1950s thousands of men worked in this area across a network of around thirty mines, producing coal for the UK's homes and factories. For nearly 200 years coal had been king in the Dearne Valley. Historically, the vast majority of jobs in the immediate vicinity were involved in coal mining or industries heavily reliant on coal such as the production of chemicals and steel. The closure of the pits in the late '80s and early '90s had a devastating impact on the region. Jobs disappeared almost overnight and the dreams and aspirations of thousands were shattered. Unemployment rose and the land around what is now the TPT lay under a coating of coal dust neglected, derelict and disused.

Slowly but surely the area is starting to recover from the collapse of the coal mining industry and from the desolation of the early '90s. The story is now one of regeneration, diversification and investment. Over the years various agencies have won significant amounts of money, which they have invested in a range of projects designed to improve the environmental and social conditions of the area. In 1991 the Dearne Valley Partnership secured around £40 million from the City Challenge and this money was augmented by other funds from the Derelict Land Grant Scheme, with some of the money being used to reclaim 1,000 acres of poor quality farmland and grassy wetlands from the old Wath Manvers Colliery complex. A pocket of 250 acres of this land, known locally as Wath Ings, was eventually earmarked for what is now the RSPB Old Moor Nature Reserve.

The RSPB Old Moor Nature Reserve attracts thousands of visitors each year and is open daily 9.30am to 5pm February to October and 9.30am to 4pm November to January. The centre has a café, which is open at all times of the year. In common with the National Wildflower Centre in Liverpool and the Catalyst Centre at Widnes, the RSPB Old Moor Nature Reserve is definitely worth a return visit. You can expect to see numerous species of birds, including great crested and little grebes, common snipes, common redshanks, lapwings, black-headed gulls, barn owls, little owls, stonechats, and tree sparrows. In winter the sky resounds with a cacophony of bird song produced by hundreds of lapwings and thousands of golden plovers. In summer look out for oystercatchers,

Stage 3: Wentworth Castle to Selby

RSPB Old Moor.

Bittern. (Photo: Geoff Haynes)

Stage 3: Wentworth Castle to Selby

Kingfisher. (Photo: Ray King)

ringed and little ringed plovers, cuckoos, yellow wagtails as well as sedge and reed warblers. Another compelling reason to return to Old Moor is to observe the bittern, one of the most threatened birds in the UK. It is a member of the heron family and is a very secretive and exceptionally well camouflaged bird, which means that it can move among the reed beds searching for fish almost unnoticed. If the bittern is disturbed it will stand motionless, its tawny brown markings helping it blend in with the waterside vegetation.

The stream immediately outside the gates of the RSPB Old Moor Nature Reserve and parallel to the TPT is a place where you might be lucky enough to catch sight of a kingfisher. You are probably familiar with this small brightly coloured bird about the size of a sparrow with a large head and a long, sharp, pointed beak. The kingfisher will fly close to the water in a blaze of iridescent blue and orange.

From RSPB Old Moor Nature Reserve continue onwards and after approximately 8.7 miles from today's start at the Wentworth Castle turning you will

Stage 3: Wentworth Castle to Selby

reach Dearne Road (**SE 448 020**). Continue to follow the TPT NCN 62 signs for a further 2.1 miles to reach Harlington village. You should now have completed approximately 10.8 miles of your journey towards Selby.

As you enter Harlington village turn right into Doncaster Road (**SE 479 026**) and follow the signs for the TPT. Cycle along Doncaster Road and you will pass Harlington Village Stores (18 Doncaster Road DN5 7HT, tel. 01709 893 311) (**SE 480 026**), which is an opportune place to stock up with snacks and sandwiches. Continue onwards, passing the Harlington Inn (01709 892 300), and at the nearby junction of Doncaster Road and Mill Lane bear right following signs for the TPT (**SE 482 024**). Cycle along Mill Lane for approximately 0.4 miles to join a further off-road section of the TPT as the trail follows the trackbed of a former railway line. Continue along this section of the trail for approximately 0.9 miles to reach Pastures Road. Turn right (**SE 498 009**), then immediately left, and once again you will be cycling off-road on the TPT. Continue onwards for a further 1.2 miles and you will now have exceptional views of Conisbrough Castle on your right.

CONISBROUGH CASTLE

One of the undoubted highlights of cycling the TPT is catching your first sight of Conisbrough Castle, which dominates the valley and inspired Sir Walter Scott's novel *Ivanhoe*. There has been a settlement in this area for over 1,000 years and the early name for what we now call Conisbrough was *Cyningesburh*, Anglo Saxon for 'the defended burh of the king'. This suggests that in the period well before the Norman Conquest an Anglo Saxon king held the area. Records from 1000–4 confirm that Wulfric, a minister to King Edward, granted the lands around 'Kyningesburg' to Elfheim, a Saxon nobleman. Six decades later at the time of the Norman invasion, the manor of Conisbrough was in the possession of King Harold, who met his fate at the Battle of Hastings. The victor King William, Duke of Normandy, gave the estate to his son-in-law, William de Warrene, who became the first Earl Warrene. Two decades later, in the Domesday survey of 1086, Conisbrough was recorded as a substantial estate comprising what we now know as the town itself and twenty other villages in the area.

It is believed that the post-conquest Norman castle at Conisbrough

Stage 3: Wentworth Castle to Selby

The magnificent keep at Conisbrough Castle.

Stage 3: Wentworth Castle to Selby

was built on a fortified earth mound topped by a wooden stockade, and in 1180 Hamelin Plantagenet, the fifth earl, raised the stone castle that we see today on the site of the earlier fortification. Over the ensuing years the castle saw visits from important figures such as King John in 1201 and King Edward II in 1322. However, the castle gradually fell out of use and was in such poor condition that by 1538 it had fallen into a state of almost total ruin and was indefensible. King Henry VIII granted the remains of the castle to the Carey family, who became its long-term custodians. In the 1940s Conisbrough Council stepped in and purchased the castle and it is now under the stewardship of English Heritage.

The castle's former political importance as a stronghold of regional power is reflected in its size and construction, and today it survives as an exceptional example of mid-medieval architecture. At the centre is the keep, which is polygonal in shape and built from limestone ashlar. The keep stands 90 feet high on a sturdy conical-shaped foundation and is supported by six massive semi-hexagonal buttresses. The keep would have been the most important part of the castle, providing a place of sanctuary and security for the resident nobility in the event of an attack. It would have served as a prison for captured enemies, while also containing a strong room for precious documents and treasure. Although it is just over a mile from the TPT, the castle is definitely worth a visit. Opening times vary as to the time of year so it is worth checking the castle website for details.

CONISBROUGH VIADUCT

From Conisbrough Castle continue onwards along the TPT for a further 0.4 miles and after approximately 14.3 miles into the third day's journey you will encounter the impressive Conisbrough Viaduct (**SK 521 996**) spanning the River Don, which used to carry the Dearne Valley railway. With its twenty-one arches, fourteen to the west and seven to the east, it is a feat of engineering. The main building contractor on the viaduct was Henry Lovatt of Wolverhampton, who engaged the services of Henderson's of Aberdeen to erect an aerial ropeway known as a 'blondin', which was slung between two 80-foot towers on each side of the valley and then used to haul materials and loads of up to three tons from one side to the other. In its day the 'blondin' was a state of the art

Stage 3: Wentworth Castle to Selby

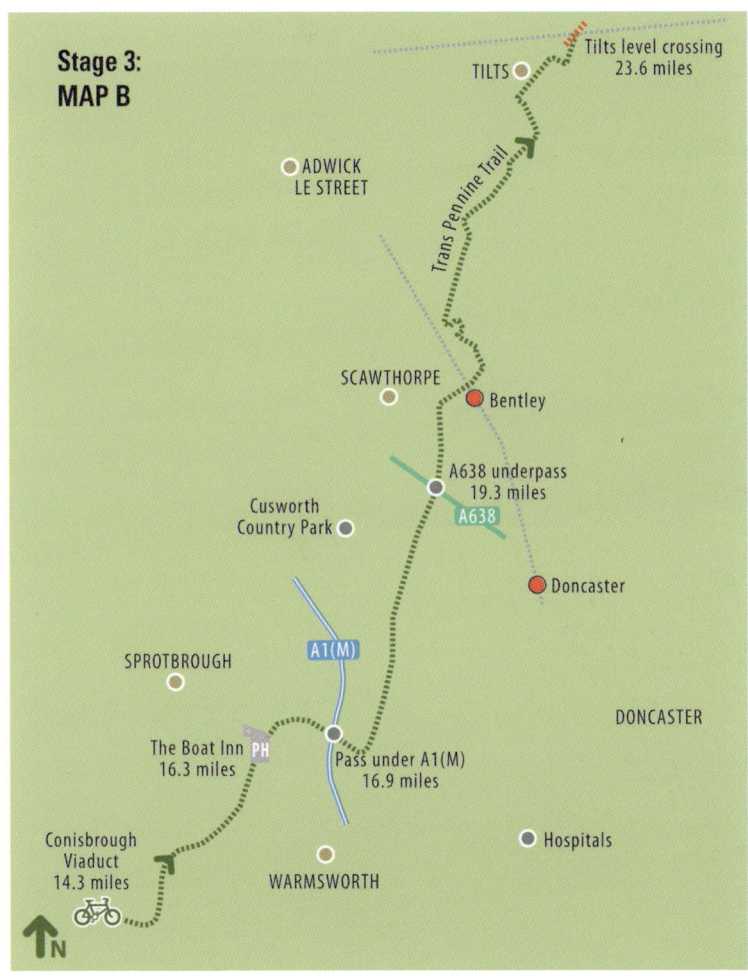

construction technique, previously used to great effect to span the Victoria Falls Bridge over the River Zambezi. During the course of the construction project on the viaduct, over 12 million bricks, 40,000 cubic feet of timber and 3,000 tons of cement were used. The viaduct was in use from 17 March 1909 before closing on 11 July 1966.

Stage 3: Wentworth Castle to Selby

Construction of Conisbrough Viaduct, 1906–07. (Photos: Keith Butcher)

Stage 3: Wentworth Castle to Selby

Against the impressive backdrop of the viaduct, continue on the off-road section of the TPT for a further 2 miles to reach the Boat Inn (**SE 536 014**), a friendly country pub approximately 16.3 miles from the day's start point at the Wentworth Castle turning at Dodworth Bottom. Cycle on from the Boat Inn following TPT NCN 62 signs for a further 3 miles to reach an underpass on the A638 York Road (**SE 559 045**) at Bentley to the north-west of Doncaster. You will now have completed around 19.3 miles of your journey. Continue onwards on the off-road NCN 62 and after approximately 0.6 miles turn right (**SE 559 055**) into Pipering Lane East and cycle on for 0.3 miles to the railway level crossing at Bentley (**SE 563 056**). Keep going for 0.1 miles along Church Street and Cooke Street before turning left into Truman Street. On the corner of Truman Street and Cooke Street (**SE 565 059**) you will find Stop n' Snack (tel. 01302 873216). This is a convenient place for a cup of tea and is open every day of the week except Sunday.

From Stop n' Snack cycle down Truman Street for 0.2 miles and turn right into Park Road and immediately left. You will have Bentley Park on your right as you head out towards more open countryside. Follow the TPT NCN 62 signs for a further 2 miles and rejoin the sealed road surface at Shaftholme Lane (**SE 571 086**). At this point turn left and cycle on for 0.3 miles before turning right into Hall Villa Lane (**SE 569 090**). Cycle along Hall Villa Lane for 0.7 miles, crossing over Tilts Drain before arriving at a railway level crossing (**SE 575 097**). The level crossing is close to the hamlet of Tilts, which is approximately 23.6 miles from this morning's start point at the Wentworth Castle signpost.

Having crossed the railway line, continue onwards for approximately 0.8 miles through the peaceful and unspoilt Owston Wood to reach Middle Lane and then turn right (**SE 576 109**). Continue onwards for 0.4 miles and again cross the railway line at Thorpe Gates (**SE 580 105**). Cycle for a matter of 0.1 miles to cross a further railway line at Joan Croft Junction (**SE 583 105**). This final railway line crossing comes after 24.9 miles into your journey. From the railway crossing continue onwards for 4 miles following the TPT NCN 62 signs to reach the village of Braithwaite (**SE 616 125**). At this stage of the journey you will have cycled 28.9 miles from this morning's starting point.

Upon leaving the village bear left into Braithwaite Lane and continue onwards for 0.2 miles to reach the off-road section of the TPT NCN 62 (**SE 621 126**), which runs alongside the New Junction Canal, for a relaxing 3.3 mile canal-side ride to Sykehouse Road Bridge (**SE 644 174**). This marks 32.4 miles of today's journey. Leave the New Junction Canal and turn left into Sykehouse Road and cycle onwards along Sykehouse Road, into Broad Lane. After 1.1 miles from leaving the canal turn right (**SE 627 167**) into Starkbridge Lane, following TPT

Stage 3: Wentworth Castle to Selby

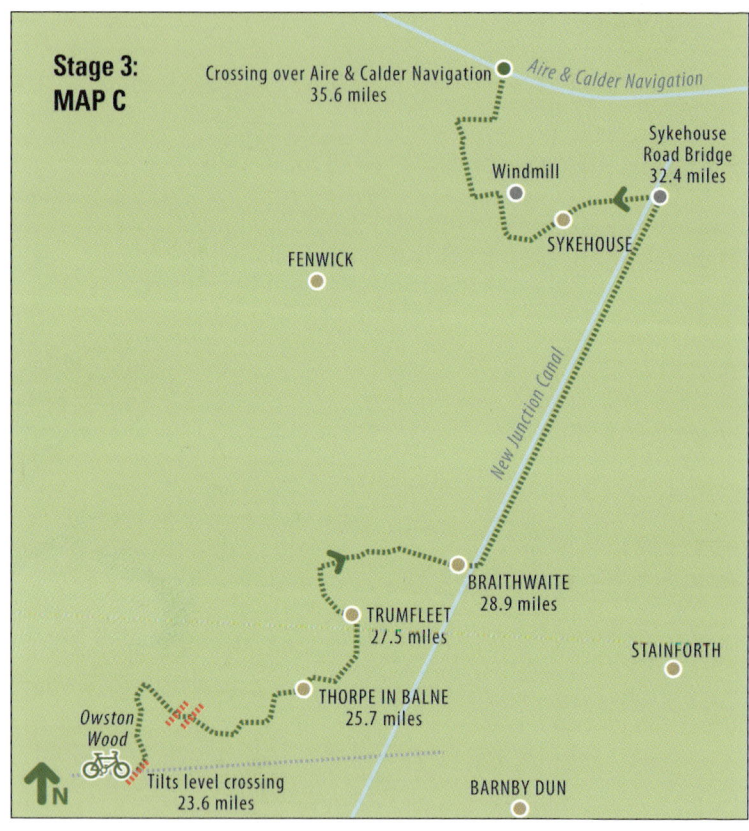

signs for Selby and Pollington. Follow the TPT signs through the back lanes for 2.1 miles and cross the Aire and Calder Navigation (**SE 624 189**) close to the village of Pollington. You will now have cycled 35.6 miles from today's start point at the Wentworth Castle signpost. (At this stage in the journey you will need to change your map to Ordnance Survey Sheet 105: York and Selby.)

Having crossed the Aire and Calder Navigation, take the immediate left fork into Cowcroft Lane and cycle for 2.1 miles, at which point you will go under the M62 motorway. This marks approximately 36.8 miles from the start of today's ride. Cycle for a further 0.2 miles to the junction with the A645 Pontefract Road and turn left (**SE 624 212**). At the A645 Pontefract Road continue for 0.4 miles

Stage 3: Wentworth Castle to Selby

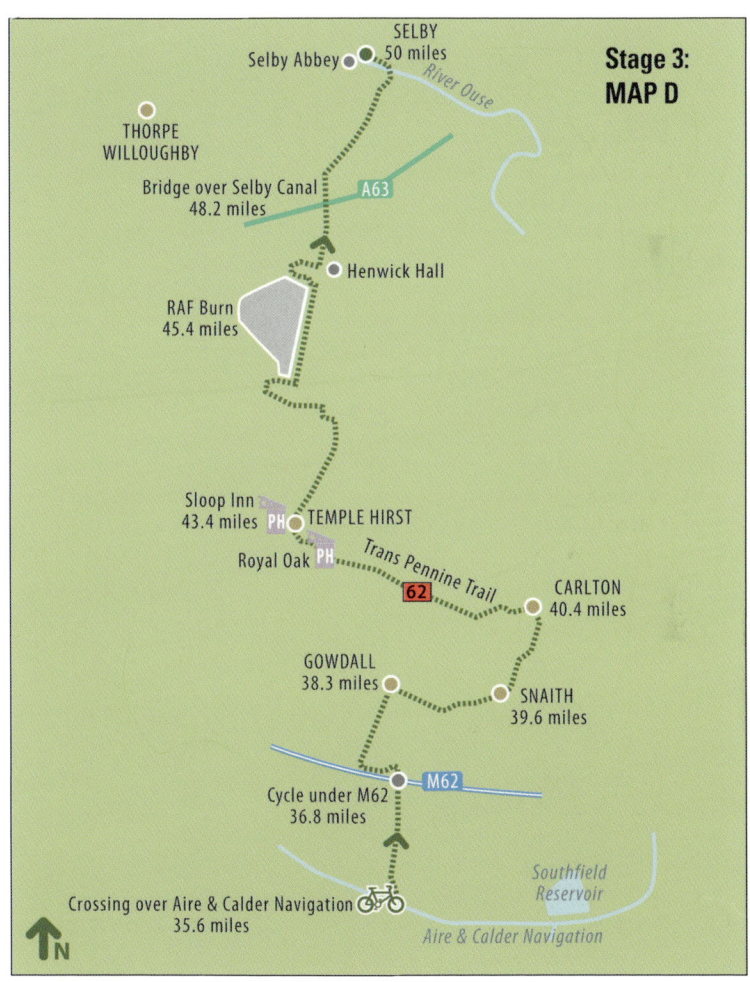

and turn right into Field Lane (**SE 618 211**). Continue along Field Lane for 0.9 miles to the junction of Main Street, Gowdall, and turn right (**SE 623 225**). Cycle from this junction for 1.3 miles into Snaith (**SE 643 224**), which is approximately 39.6 miles into today's journey. Once at the junction of the A1041, Ferry Lane, Snaith, turn left following TPT signs and signs for Carlton and Drax. Cycle along

Stage 3: Wentworth Castle to Selby

the A1041 Ferry Lane for 0.8 miles and then turn left into Low Street, Carlton (**SE 647 235**). You should now have completed approximately 40.4 miles from the start point at the Wentworth Castle turning at Dodworth Bottom.

Continue along Low Street for 0.3 miles, turn left onto Hirst Road (**SE 646 237**) and cycle along Hirst Road for 2.2 miles to reach The Royal Oak (**SE 610 246**). This village pub also has a small campsite, which charges £10 per night for a tent and two persons. From the Royal Oak pub continue for a further 0.3 miles to the Sloop Inn (**SE 606 248**). This pub also has a small campsite (tel. 01757 270 267).

Cycle on for 0.2 miles from the Sloop Inn and turn right (**SE 605 250**). At this point you will have travelled approximately 43.4 miles from the start at Wentworth Castle. Take care: this right turn is easy to miss. Having turned right continue along a very quiet country lane for approximately 2 miles and you should find yourself at the entrance to a former airfield, RAF Burn (**SE 602 272**). You will have cycled 45.4 miles from the start of today's ride. Turn right at this point and traverse the southern section of the airfield for 0.3 miles heading towards the railway line. You should then turn left and follow the TPT NCN 62 north for approximately 1.1 miles, keeping the railway line to your right.

Traces of the old runway at former RAF Burn.

Stage 3: Wentworth Castle to Selby

RAF BURN

In its day RAF Burn was one of a clutch of wartime airfields surrounding the town of Selby. During the Second World War, the skies over this part of Yorkshire would have been crowded with military aircraft. The history of the airfield goes back to 1940 when Great Britain was fighting for her very survival, with land at Burn requisitioned for the construction of an airfield which would allow heavy bombers to take off whatever the direction of the wind.

The building of the runways and the 230 ancillary buildings began in the winter of 1941 and even before the construction work had been completed in the summer and autumn of 1942 RAF Burn was turned over to 1653 Royal Air Force Conversion Unit. These airmen were updating their skills and converting to fly heavy Liberator bombers for operational sorties in the Middle East. With training completed by the end of October 1942 RAF Burn was then operationally assigned to 431 Squadron of the Royal Canadian Air Force, who flew Wellington bombers that were mainly engaged in bombing and mine laying. The Canadians departed in July 1943, at which point there was a lull in operational activity that lasted until the winter of 1944. The relative calm was interrupted with the arrival of 578 Squadron, who were equipped with Halifax bombers. With the arrival of this squadron RAF Burn was once again back at full operational capacity, acting as a key base from which the Allies were able to launch bombing raids on Berlin and other German cities, as well as targeting the politically important Bavarian city of Nuremberg.

It was during a raid deep into the heart of Bavaria on 30 March 1944 that one young pilot officer based at RAF Burn named Cyril Joe Barton, aged twenty-two, made the ultimate sacrifice for his country. Barton gave his life in pursuit of his mission. He was the pilot and captain of a Handley Page Halifax Mark III bomber, serial number LK 797, which the crew had nicknamed Excalibur. The Halifax and its crew formed part of a huge Allied raid involving nearly 800 aircraft attacking Nuremberg. Around seventy miles short of the target Excalibur came under sustained attack from a Junkers 88 and a Messerschmitt 210. The Nazi assault destroyed the plane's intercom, inflicted serious damage to the engine and rendered Excalibur's machine guns inoperable, meaning that returning fire

Stage 3: Wentworth Castle to Selby

was impossible. In the confusion and maelstrom of the Nazi onslaught, instructions were misunderstood and the navigator, wireless operator and air bomber baled out of the stricken Halifax.

Bravely, Barton pushed on, as he was determined to see the mission through. Excalibur and its remaining crew were highly vulnerable to further attack as the aircraft was silhouetted against the night sky by the ruins of Nuremberg burning below. The indomitable Barton and his crew pressed the attack home and released their deadly payload before finally wheeling the Halifax around and heading back in the direction of RAF Burn. With the navigator gone, Barton took on navigational duties and using a chart in the cockpit and the Pole Star he set a course back to England. The homeward passage proved to be a horrendous journey that saw the captain and the remaining crew fight for every mile. Their aircraft was buffeted in the teeth of a brutal head wind, they lost a propeller and two fuel tanks began to leak badly. It was only through Barton's exceptional courage and flying skills that he managed to make landfall just ninety miles north of RAF Burn. By now Excalibur was spent and rapidly losing altitude. In a final selfless act, Barton managed to prevent the Halifax coming down in a heavily populated area, although it eventually crashed at Ryhope Colliery near Sunderland, where Barton was killed. Miraculously, three of his comrades survived. In recognition of his courage and gallantry in the face of almost impossible odds Barton was posthumously awarded the Victoria Cross (VC) by King George VI. The VC is the highest military decoration that can be bestowed for valour in the face of the enemy.

Almost a year after Barton's death, 578 Squadron had been stood down from RAF Burn. They had flown 2,722 sorties, been involved in 161 operations against 107 enemy targets, lost 46 aircraft and 219 of their airmen were killed. In addition to Barton's VC, members of 578 Squadron earned numerous awards for courage and exemplary service including two Distinguished Service Orders, 143 Distinguished Flying Crosses and 79 Distinguished Flying Medals. Today Cyril Barton and his comrades of 578 Squadron are remembered forever at a memorial stone in Burn village and also within Selby Abbey, where a plaque is dedicated to Flying Officer Cyril Joe Barton, VC, RAFVR and Wing Commander David Wilkerson, DSO, DFC, RAFVR. Cyril Barton's hard-won and deserved VC can currently be found at the Royal Air Force Museum.

Stage 3: Wentworth Castle to Selby

From the old RAF base at Burn you will find Selby is almost within sight. Having cycled to the northern edge of the runway (**SE 609 289**), bear left and cycle for 0.3 miles. Then turn right and cycle for approximately 100 yards before taking the TPT NCN 62 by turning right onto Common Lane (**SE 605 291**). You should then cycle for 0.3 miles to reach Henwick Hall Lane (**SE 609 291**). Turn left and cycle along Henwick Hall Lane for 0.7 miles to go under the A63 (**SE 610 302**).

From going under the A63, cycle onwards for a further 0.2 miles to reach the junction with Brayton Lane where you should turn left and cycle for a mere 75 yards to the bridge over the Selby Canal (**SE 610 304**). At this point you will have cycled approximately 48.2 miles from the start point at the Wentworth Castle signpost. All that remains is to cycle alongside the Selby Canal on the TPT NCN 62 for a further 1.7 miles into Selby town centre (**SE 615 325**), where there is a whole range of accommodation. The total mileage for today's ride is 50 miles.

SELBY ABBEY

The third stage of the TPT route described in this guidebook concludes in Selby and we would urge the reader to take a little time to pay a visit to Selby Abbey, the Church of Our Lord, St Mary and St Germain, founded in 1069. It is regarded as one of the finest non-cathedral parish churches in the country. Besides the architectural splendour of the building, the monastic legend surrounding the early history of the abbey is enthralling. Selby Abbey emerged as an offshoot of the eminent Benedictine Abbey at Auxerre, south-east of Paris. The founding of Selby Abbey appears to have been a combination of political good fortune and the persistence of a young French monk called Benedict.

The records tell us that young Benedict had been brought up within the abbey at Auxerre and originally served the abbot in a secular rather than religious role. As he grew older Benedict had career choices to make to become a knight or a monk. Benedict chose the latter, dedicating himself to a life of religious service within the Benedictine order. As Benedict readied himself for a lifetime of prayer and contemplation, William the Conqueror invaded England. Benedict remained in France doing well in his work, becoming a sacrist with responsibility for the religious relics held in the abbey. The course of Benedict's life was altered forever when he was visited in a series of three dreams by St Germain, the patron saint of the abbey. Each dream had a similar theme: that Benedict should leave the abbey and found a religious community in St Germain's honour. Benedict was reluctant to act, yet in the third and final dream St Germain forcefully warned Benedict of the dire consequences, should he fail to carry out his wishes.

*Selby Abbey.
(Photo: Rev. Canon
J. Weetman and
Martyn Weaver)*

On the horns of a dilemma, Benedict asked the prior's permission to take leave of the abbey, which was refused. Benedict fled in the dead of night, taking with him a valuable religious relic, the preserved middle finger from the right hand of St Germain. Pursued by his brothers from the monastery at Auxerre, he made for the coast and took a ship to England. Either by a misunderstanding or misinterpretation, Benedict made his way to Salisbury where he received another vision from the saint instructing him to head north and go to Selby.

Benedict made his way north, making a further passage by ship from Kings Lynn to York before finally sailing up the River Ouse and landing at Selby. Benedict recognized the place from his vision and the sight of three swans on the water, which he interpreted as a sign of the Holy Trinity, confirmed that Selby was the correct location in which to start the community. Benedict erected a cross and set up a small oratory on the banks of the river while sheltering under a magnificent oak tree that the locals named Strihac.

Benedict, a stranger and a pilgrim, had arrived in England at a time of great tumult. He had also taken a great risk by setting up his community without permission. In the wake of the Norman Conquest this region was a savage and inhospitable place, with the locals fighting an insurgency against the Norman invaders. Benedict's diminutive religious community on the banks of the River Ouse was also attracting attention, not least from Hugh Fitz Baldric, the Sheriff of Yorkshire, who sighted Benedict's cross as he was patrolling the river. Benedict appealed to Hugh for protection and he impressed the sheriff to such an extent that he supplied Benedict with carpenters to build a wooden chantry. The sheriff also introduced him to King William (the Conqueror), who was celebrating Christmas in York after his harrying of the north.

Stage 3: Wentworth Castle to Selby

Benedict was exceptionally fortunate because King William granted him permission to build an abbey. The ascendancy of Benedict, the rebellious monk who fled France with the saintly relic, was complete when he was ordained as the first Abbot of Selby by the Archbishop of York. With little time to waste Benedict set about acquiring more land for the abbey and by 1090 it was financially secure. Benedict added to its coffers by healing the son of Erneis de Burun using St Germain's relic, for which he received a donation of 100 marks. However, scandal visited the abbey after two recalcitrant monks stole a significant amount of treasure and fled. They were pursued by Benedict to Northampton where he ordered their castration and, when news of this brutal punishment reached the king, it was Benedict who was forced on the run as he was sought by Stephen, the abbot of St Mary's in York. Fortunately for Benedict, Stephen allowed him to escape, although it was too late for Benedict to salvage his reputation. He had lost the confidence of the king and this, coupled with the hostility from his brother monks, meant that his fall from grace was swift. He was forced to resign and ended his days as a hermit in Rochester.

The abbey church dominates the skyline of Selby and the building we see today was started by Benedict's successor Abbot Hugh de Lacey (1097–1123), who rebuilt the old wooden structure, replacing it with stone from nearby Monk Fryston. Most of the work was completed in Abbot Hugh's lifetime. However, the nave remained unfinished and it was not until AD1230 that his plans were finally completed. Selby survived the Dissolution and legally became a parish church in 1618. We know that in 1690 the central tower, which had stood for six centuries, fell down and severely damaged the southern transept. Over 200 years later, on the night of 19 and 20 October 1906, the abbey suffered its greatest calamity when a fire damaged the whole fabric of the building. Fortunately the walls remained standing but the interior was reduced to a mass of burnt timber and melted lead. The people of Selby were quick to react and a restoration fund was begun. It took two years before the crossing tower was rebuilt. The upper stages of the western towers were replaced a few years later and by 1935 Selby Abbey looked as it once had in Norman times.

In the twenty-first century Selby Abbey remains a magnificent sight. It has stood firm as the challenges of each passing era have come to its doors, surviving the political tumult of the Dissolution of the Monasteries, the armies of Oliver Cromwell and Charles I, and the fire of 1906. The latest challenge for the abbey is financial rather than political in that the custodians are faced with the yearly task of raising around £350,000 to ensure the upkeep of the building to a standard that is demanded of a world-renowned abbey and important place of worship for its local congregation.

STAGE 4:

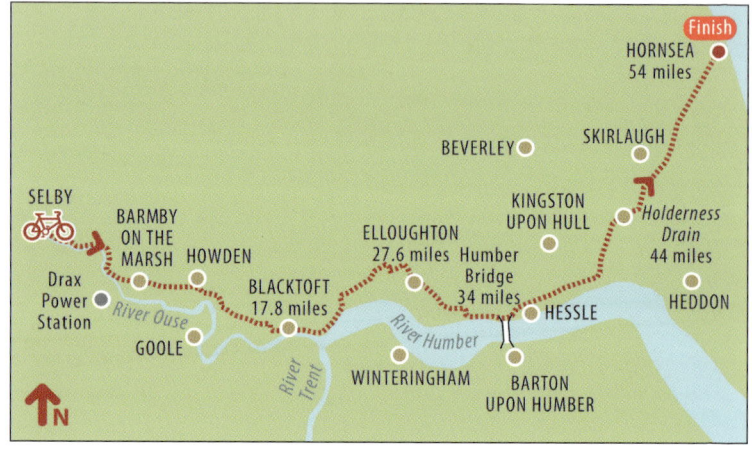

54 miles
Terrain: Flat

Maps required:
Ordnance Survey Landranger Sheet 105: York and Selby
Ordnance Survey Landranger Sheet 106: Market Weighton
Ordnance Survey Landranger Sheet 107: Kingston upon Hull

SELBY TO HORNSEA

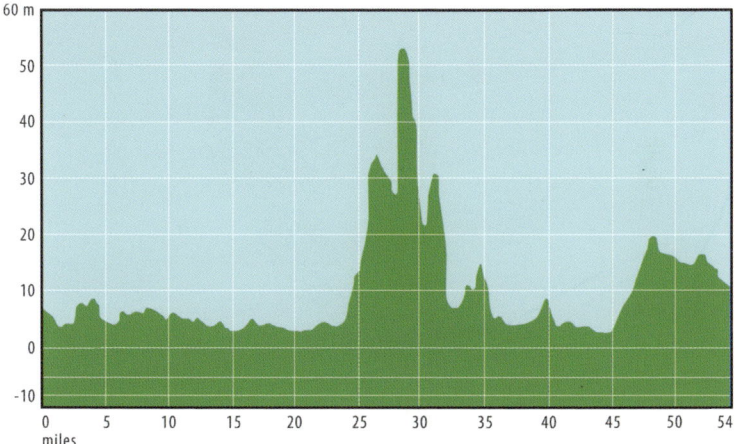

A good place to begin the fourth and final day of the cycle tour is from the north bank of the River Ouse in Barlby Road (**SE 617 326**), just over the bridge in the centre of Selby. The start of the ride is immediately outside Temperance House and from this point you should cycle along the TPT NCN 65 signed towards Howden. Continue along Ouse Bank at the side of the River Ouse and after 1.2 miles you will go under the A63 (**SE 635 317**). From this point cycle onwards for a further 0.7 miles and follow the road to the left into Turnham Lane (**SE 645 314**). From Turnham Lane continue for 1.4 miles to reach the A63 Hull Road and turn right (**SE 666 315**). Cycle onwards from this junction into the nearby village of Hemingbrough, which marks 3.7 miles into the journey. You will find a Londis Store in Main Street, which is a handy place to stock up with sandwiches before the rest of the day unfolds. There are also two pubs in the village: the Fox and Pheasant (tel. 01757 638 327) (**SE 674 306**) and the Crown (tel. 01757 638 434) (**SE 674 304**). From Hemingbrough village you should continue onwards, passing the Church of Saint Mary the Virgin, and continue on for 1.9 miles. This part of the route is initially a lane and then an off-road section of the TPT NCN 65. You will then

Stage 4: Selby to Hornsea

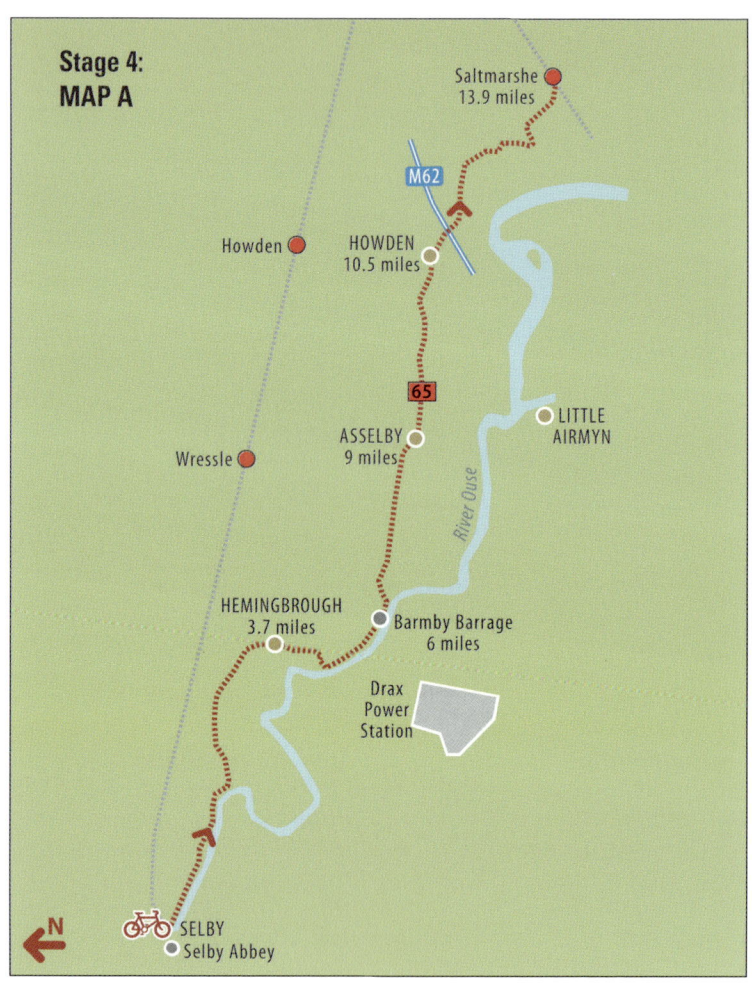

reach Barmby Barrrage on the River Ouse (**SE 680 286**) and will have cycled 6 miles from the start point in Selby.

Leave Barmby Barrage and cycle for 0.5 miles to reach the Kings Head (tel. 01757 630 705). Continue for a further 2.5 miles into the village of Asselby (**SE 718 281**) and onwards for a further 1.1 miles into the hamlet of Knedlington

Stage 4: Selby to Hornsea

(**SE 731 281**), where you will reach the junction of Boothferry Road, Main Street, and Knedlington Road (**SE 736 280**). This junction marks 9.6 miles of your journey. At this junction go straight over and continue along the B1228 Knedlington Road for 0.6 miles to reach Treeton Road, Howden, and turn right (**SE 746 280**) following signs for the TPT. Cycle along Treeton Road for 0.3 miles, turn right into Hailgate and continue on, negotiating the Howden Renault roundabout (**SE 752 279**) at the junction with the A614 Boothferry Road. At this point on the final day of the ride you will have cycled approximately 10.5 miles from the start point in Selby.

From the roundabout, cycle into Howden Dyke Road and continue onwards for 0.4 miles to cross the M62 (**SE 756 276**). From the crossing over the M62 cycle for 0.2 miles and turn left following signs for Kilpin 1 and Laxton 3. This junction is also notable for a TPT NCN 65 sign (**SE 758 274**). Continue along this quiet country lane for 1 mile to the junction with Mill Lane, Kilpin, and turn right (**SE 773 269**). Cycle along Mill Lane for 0.6 miles to the junction with Skelton Broad Lane (**SE 773 261**) and turn left. Cycle along this lane for 1.1 miles to reach Saltmarshe railway station (**SE 787 258**). The railway station marks approximately 13.9 miles of cycling from the start of today's ride. Cycle on from the railway station for 0.2 miles to reach the Bricklayers Arms (**SE 790 257**). At this point in the journey you should change to Ordnance Survey Sheet 106: Market Weighton.

From the pub cycle for 0.6 miles along Chapel Lane to reach the junction of Cotness Lane and Metham Lane (**SE 798 251**) and continue straight ahead along Metham Lane. You will pass Metham Hall Farm and at the next junction turn right towards Yokefleet (**SE 816 250**). From the junction continue along this peaceful lane for approximately 2 miles to reach Blacktoft Old School Hall (**SE 840 243**), which marks 17.8 miles of cycling from the start point in Selby.

From the old school hall cycle on for 0.2 miles and you will reach the Hope and Anchor (tel. 01430 440 441), a pub that enjoys an excellent reputation for food (**SE 844 242**). From the Hope and Anchor continue onwards for 1.3 miles, cycling through the hamlet of Flaxfleet (**SE 864 242**), and you will catch a glimpse of Whitton Island and the River Humber. The Humber Estuary is world-renowned for the importance of its wetland habitat and its rare ecosystem. It is also designated as a National Character Area and a European Marine Site. Many thousands of birds such as shelduck, lapwing, sanderling, pochard and brent geese make the estuary their habitat at varying times of the year. The estuary is also renowned within the world of ornithology for its rarer visitors, such as the marsh harrier and the bearded tit.

From Flaxfleet continue onwards for a further 1.2 miles, ensuring that you

Stage 4: Selby to Hornsea

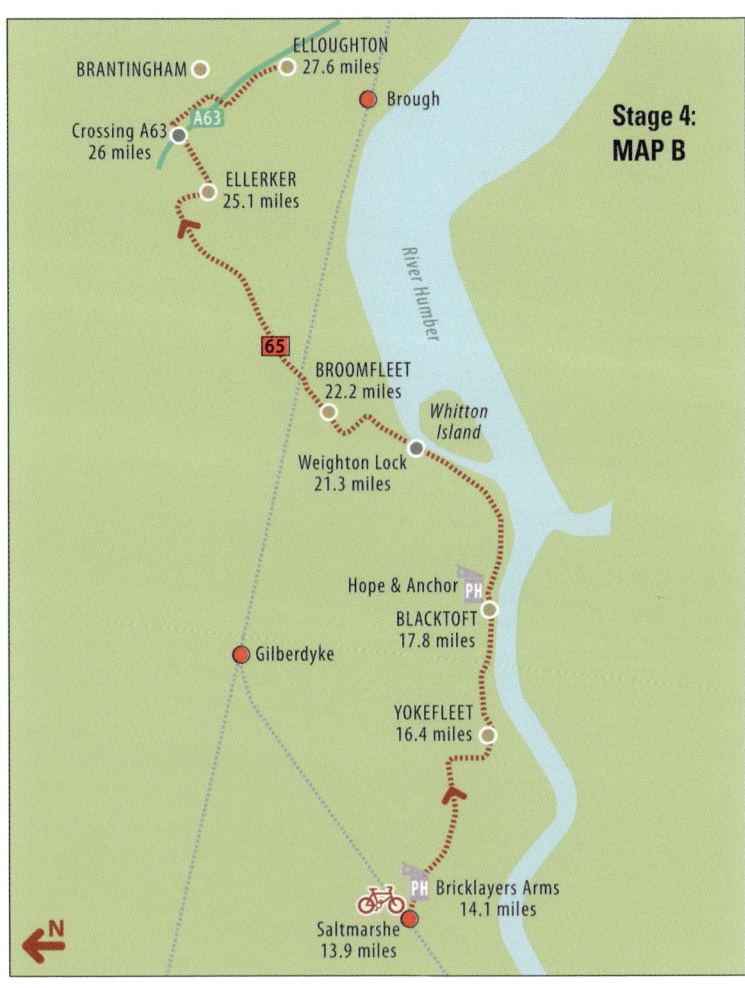

follow the TPT NCN 65 to Weighton Lock (**SE 874 256**). This particular area has a unique, peaceful feel. The sky is expansive, the light is bright and brisk winds from the estuary whip across the landscape with the horizon ever changing as clouds scud by. It was a place dearly loved by Philip Larkin, the famous post-war poet, who used to visit the area on his bicycle. Larkin's links

Stage 4: Selby to Hornsea

Big skies at Weighton Lock.

with Hull and this part of Humberside are highlighted within the innovative Larkin Trail website.

From Weighton Lock continue onwards for 0.9 miles to Main Street, Broomfleet (**SE 876 270**), where you should turn right and cycle along Main Street into the centre of the village. At this stage of the ride you will have cycled approximately 22.2 miles from this morning's start point in Selby. From the centre of Broomfleet village, cycle onwards for approximately 2.6 miles, remaining on the TPT NCN 65. You will then reach the junction of Norfolk Bank Lane, Stonepit Road and Cave Lane, where you should now turn right (**SE 919 300**). This marks approximately 24.8 miles of the journey.

Continue along Cave Lane for 0.3 miles to the junction with Main Street; follow the road around to the right and then to the left. Cycle past the Black Horse Restaurant (**SE 921 294**) and then continue straight on to reach the junction with Howden Croft Hill and turn left (**SE 922 293**). From the junction of Howden Croft Hill cycle onwards for 0.6 miles along Ring Beck Lane to the crossroads (**SE 930 297**), which is marked by its close proximity to Greens Garden Centre, and go straight over. Continue onwards for a further 0.3 miles, going over the A63 dual carriageway (**SE 933 299**), which marks 26 miles of

Stage 4: Selby to Hornsea

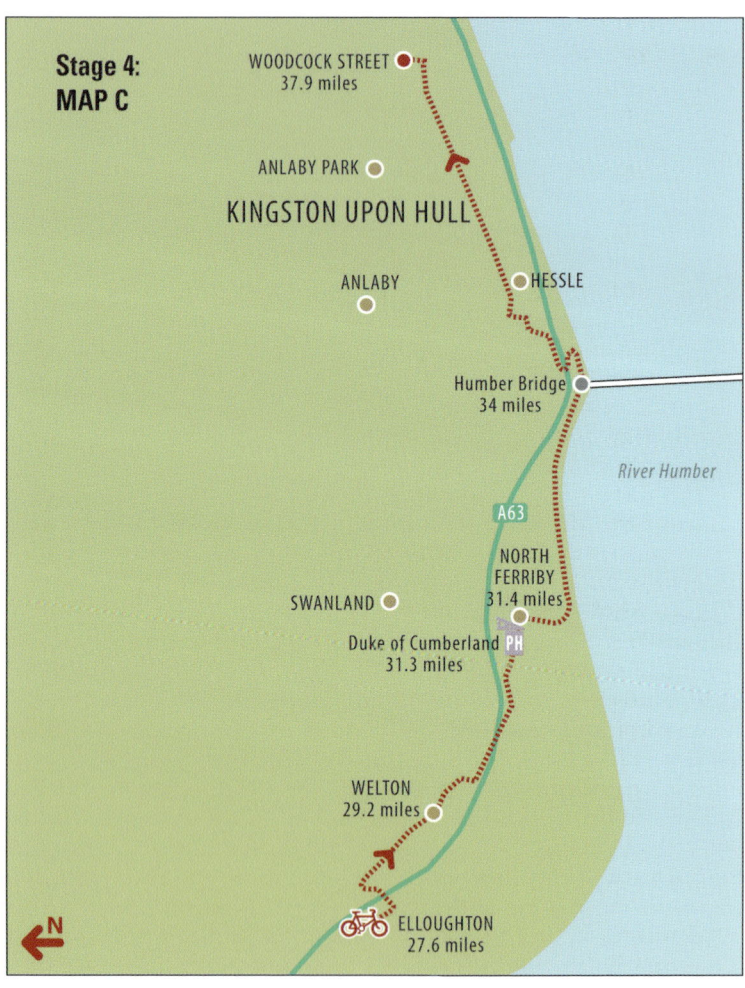

your journey today, and follow the road as it bears around to the right. As the road bears around to the right continue onwards for approximately 0.6 miles to the Triton Inn, Brantingham (**SE 938 295**). From Brantingham continue onwards for 0.2 miles, once again crossing the A63 (**SE 939 292**), before turning left and cycling for 0.8 miles to the junction of Brantingham Road and Church Street,

Stage 4: Selby to Hornsea

Elloughton (**SE 945 282**). Continue for 0.1 miles into the centre of the village (**SE 945 281**) where you will find the Half Moon Inn, which is a welcoming pub for a drink or a snack.

Go past the Half Moon Inn, cycle along Welton Low Road for 0.2 miles and turn left into Dale Road (**SE 946 278**). Cycle for 0.1 miles to again cross the A63 (**SE 948 280**); this comes 28 miles after the start of today's ride. Continue cycling along Dale Road for 0.2 miles (from crossing the A63) and turn right (**SE 948 283**) (you will still be on Dale Road). After a further 120 yards you will reach the junction of Dale Road and the High Road; turn right at this junction (**SE 950 284**). You should now cycle along High Road for 0.6 miles to reach the junction with Kidd Lane (**SE 957 276**). Continue for 0.2 miles to the junction of Kidd Lane and Parliament Street, Welton. Cycle through the village, passing a distinctive former police station in Parliament Street, Welton (**SE 959 274**). This marks 29.2 miles of the journey so far from Selby. The next stretch of cycling, although relatively flat, does require concentration as the TPT NCN 65 traverses the city of Kingston upon Hull.

Continue from the former police station along Parliament Street, Welton, and then bear left into Welton Old Road and cycle for approximately 0.4 miles to reach South Hunsley School and Sixth Form College (**SE 966 269**). Continue straight past the school, cycle on for 0.4 miles along Melton Old Road and turn right into Gibson Lane North (**SE 972 265**). Cycle down this road for approximately 100 yards and then walk over the footbridge (**SE 971 264**), which traverses the A63 dual carriageway. This footbridge is 30.2 miles from the start of the ride in Selby. From the footbridge continue to follow the TPT NCN 65 signs for approximately 1.1 miles to reach the Duke of Cumberland public house (High Street, North Ferriby HU14 3JP, tel. 01482 631592) (**SE 987 263**). At this stage of the journey you will have cycled approximately 31.3 miles from Selby.

From the Duke of Cumberland cycle for 0.1 miles to the junction of the B1231 High Street and Church Road (**SE 989 262**) and turn right. Continue along Church Road for approximately 0.5 miles, turn left (**SE 988 255**) and then cycle in the direction of the unmistakeable Humber Bridge. For those riders who may be suffering from a few aches and pains, you will find Boots the Chemist at 44 Church Road, North Ferriby. This part of the TPT is superb; you will be cycling with tremendous views of the River Humber away to the right and the iconic structure of the Humber Bridge ahead. As you leave Church Road, North Ferriby, continue along this riverside stretch of the TPT for 3.8 miles and after 34 miles from the start of your journey you will reach the Humber Bridge (**TA 024 253**). At this point you will need to change to Ordnance Survey Sheet 107: Kingston upon Hull.

Stage 4: Selby to Hornsea

The Humber Bridge.

HUMBER BRIDGE

As far back as the nineteenth century, engineering schemes were proposed to deal with crossing the River Humber. A tunnel was first mooted back in 1872–73, although it was not until 1928 that Hull City Council

Stage 4: Selby to Hornsea

gave the project a real boost by appointing Sir Douglas Fox and Partners as consulting engineers, charged with investigating the feasibility of a bridge or a tunnel. By 1935 the engineers had settled on a suspension bridge with a span of 1,372 metres, which largely corresponds to the construction that stands before you today. This type of bridge was favoured for two key reasons. Firstly, the Humber estuary has a shifting riverbed, meaning that the navigable channel changes; any supporting piers constructed in the channel would present a constant danger to shipping. Secondly, building a bridge that encompassed supporting piers would have proved enormously expensive because of the exceptionally difficult geological conditions. The suspension bridge design was therefore agreed upon, although the scheme was initially mothballed due to the intervention of the Second World War.

In 1955 the issue of bridging the Humber was revisited and by 1959 an Act of Parliament led to the inauguration of the Humber Bridge Board, who were given the power to finance, construct, operate and collect tolls on the crossing. Construction on the suspension bridge commenced in 1972 and it proved to be a real challenge. From the outset the project was beset with difficulties. Severe weather, increasing construction costs and the complicated engineering challenge of founding the south pier in the treacherous clay on the Barton bank all conspired to put the project way behind schedule. While the original estimated cost of the bridge was conservatively put at £16 million, by the time Queen Elizabeth II finally opened the crossing on 17 July 1981 the cost had risen to an eye-watering £151 million, mostly caused by rising construction costs and interest charges. Three decades later the debt had almost doubled to a colossal £330 million.

Attempts were made to reduce the deficit with high crossing tolls being levied on motorists and hauliers. This stirred up further controversy, with politicians arguing that these charges were damaging the local economy. In March 2012 the government finally acted, stepping in and writing off £150 million of the debt and lowering the toll for cars from £3 to £1.50. Notwithstanding the huge construction costs and the saga of the debt and toll charges, the Humber Bridge remains a momentous feat of engineering and has been described as 'technically perfect'. It boasts an enormous main span of 1,410 metres and for nearly two decades it was the longest single span suspension bridge anywhere in the world.

Stage 4: Selby to Hornsea

Construction of the Humber Bridge. (Photos: Professor Niels Gimsing)

Stage 4: Selby to Hornsea

Cycle on from the Humber Bridge along Cliff Road and after 0.3 miles bear left and continue for 0.1 miles to the junction of Cliff Road and Redcliff Road (**TA 027 255**), where you should turn right and continue onwards for a further 0.4 miles to reach San Luca Italian Restaurant (**TA 034 256**). This restaurant is approximately 34.8 miles from the start point in Selby. From San Luca cycle for 0.6 miles to reach Priory Way (**TA 044 260**). Cross the A63 and cycle for 0.3 miles to Sainsbury's supermarket. This store has a cáfe, which is open Monday to Friday 8am to 10pm and Saturday 7am to 10pm, while on Sunday it is open from 10am to 4pm. From Sainsbury's continue on for a further 0.2 miles to reach Hessle Road (**TA 045 265**). This junction is marked by a communications aerial within the compound of Humberside Fire and Rescue Service and is approximately 35.9 miles from the start at Selby. You should then continue along Hessle Road for approximately 1.8 miles towards the city centre and look out for the Dairycoates Inn public house and Lidl supermarket as important navigational landmarks. Continue for a further 120 yards from Lidl and turn *left* into St Nectan Close (**TA 073 276**); this marks approximately 37.7 miles from the start of today's ride.

Having cycled into St Nectan Close, continue straight on for 100 yards and bear right into Dairycoates Avenue following the TPT sign. Cycle along Dairycoates Avenue for 0.2 miles to reach the junction of Dairycoates Avenue and Woodcock Street and then turn right (**TA 074 279**). Having turned right into Woodcock Street, continue onwards and cycle into Gordon Street and at the junction of Gordon Street and the Boulevard you will come across an ornate fountain (**TA 079 281**). The fountain is approximately 38.4 miles from the start in Selby. From the fountain cycle straight ahead and along Cholmley Street for 0.2 miles and turn left at the end of Cholmley Street (**TA 082 284**) into Coltman Street. Cycle onwards for 100 yards and turn *right,* following the TPT NCN 1/65 cycle path signs that are placed adjacent to the NHS Day Services Mental Health building. Follow the TPT to the side of the NHS building and along Bean Street for 0.1 mile to reach Rawling Way (**TA 083 284**). At this point cross over Rawling Way and continue to follow the TPT signs. You will then be cycling into Harthill Drive and Great Thornton Street to reach the staggered junction with Icehouse Road and Walker Street. The journey from crossing Rawling Way to Icehouse Road (**TA 088 286**) is approximately 0.4 miles.

At the staggered junction of Icehouse Road and Walker Street go straight ahead into Icehouse Road, cycle for 60 yards and bear left into Cambridge Street, following signs for the TPT NCN 1/65. Continue along Cambridge Street for 0.1 miles to the junction of Cambridge Street and Pease Street (**TA 090 286**). Turn right into Pease Street and cycle for 60 yards to the junction of St Luke's Street

Stage 4: Selby to Hornsea

and turn left. Cycle along St Luke's Street for 120 yards to reach a roundabout at the junction of St Luke's Street, Osborne Street, Midland Street and Porter Street. Then cycle straight on into Osborne Street and continue for a further 150 yards to reach the junction with the A1079 Ferensway (**TA 093 286**). This intersection occurs after approximately 39.4 miles from the start of the day's ride at Selby.

At the junction of Osborne Street cycle across the busy A1079 Ferensway, continue along Osborne Street and after 100 yards turn left into Ann Street (**TA 094 286**). Cycle along Ann Street for 100 yards and then turn right into Carr Lane (**TA 094 288**). From the junction of Ann Street and Carr Lane cycle

Stage 4: Selby to Hornsea

along Carr Lane for 0.1 miles to the Punch Hotel. Opposite the hotel you will find a Sustrans marker and in adjoining Paragon Street you will find Hull Tourist Information Office (**TA 095 288**), which is open daily between 10am and 5pm and on Sunday between 11am and 3pm (tel. 01482 223559). The Sustrans marker is 39.6 miles from the start of the ride in Selby.

From the Sustrans marker cycle straight on while remaining on Carr Lane. After approximately 120 yards you will cycle past the Streetlife Museum of Transport to your left. Continue onwards from the Streetlife Museum for 70 yards to the junction of Carr Lane and Queens Dock Avenue and turn right (**TA 097 287**). Now cycle along Queens Dock Avenue for a mere 50 yards and then continue straight on, cycling along Alfred Gelder Street for approximately 0.3 miles to reach the junction of Alfred Gelder Street, Clarence Street and the High Street. At this point cycle straight ahead for 100 yards to reach the unmistakeable Drypool Bridge at Clarence Street that spans the River Hull (**TA 103 289**). At the this point in the final day's cycling you will have covered approximately 40.1 miles from the start point in Selby.

From Drypool Bridge, Clarence Street, cycle on for 0.4 miles to the junction of the A165 Witham and Holderness Road and go straight across this junction into Dansom Lane South (**TA 107 294**). You should now cycle along Dansom Lane South and after 0.2 miles from the junction with Witham and Holderness Road turn left and follow the TPT sign (**TA 107 295**). The left turn is 40.7 miles from the start at Selby. You will now be cycling on the TPT NCN 65, a traffic-free ride along the trackbed of the former Hull to Hornsea railway line out of the city centre. As you cycle from the city, after approximately 3.2 miles from joining the off-road section of the TPT NCN 65, you will reach Holderness Drain (**TA 125 342**).

Continue onwards from Holderness Drain and after approximately 2.8 miles you will reach the A165 Oubrough Lane (**TA 154 375**). This marks 46.8 miles from the start at Selby. Gardeners Country Inn (tel. 01964 562625) is approximately 0.3 miles from crossing the A165 at Oubrough Lane and is a lovely place for a cold drink on a hot summer's afternoon.

Take care crossing the road and continue along the TPT NCN 65 for approximately 1.7 miles to reach Lambwath Lane, New Ellerby (**TA 168 395**). At this stage of the journey you will have completed around 48.3 miles of cycling and at New Ellerby you will find the Railway Inn (tel. 01964 563 770). You are now only a few miles away from the conclusion of four days of tremendous cycling. Remain on the TPT NCN 65 from New Ellerby and cycle onwards towards Hornsea. Continue along the TPT NCN 65 for 4.8 miles to reach the roundabout at the junction of Southgate and Rolston Road (**TA 203 469**) and from this

Stage 4: Selby to Hornsea

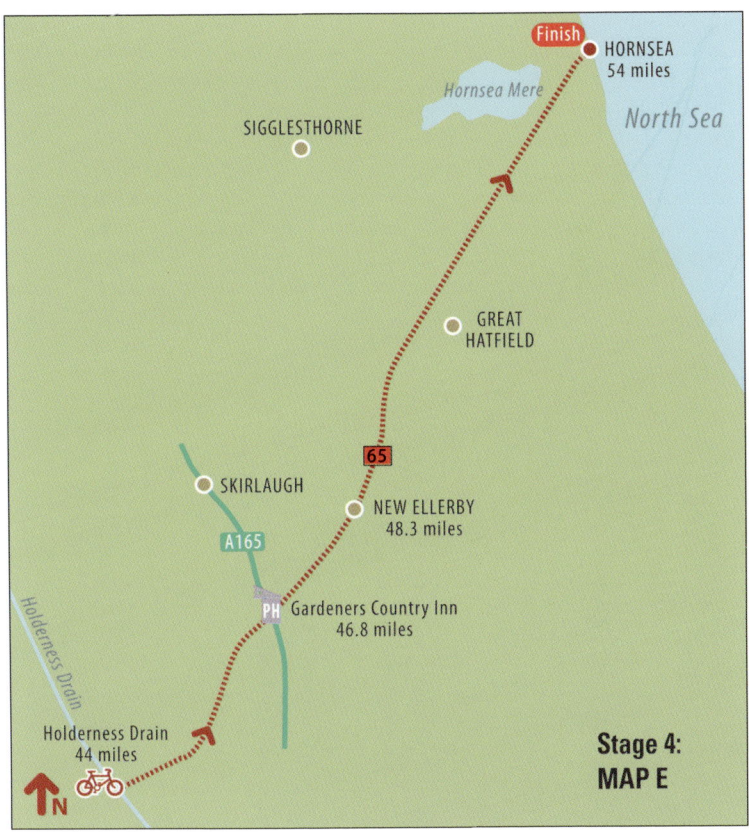

junction follow the TPT NCN 65 signs for approximately 1 mile to the junction with Sands Lane. At this intersection you will find an interesting cylindrical TPT marker opposite the old Hornsea railway station. You should now bear right and cycle the final 400 yards to the finish line, which is marked by the unmissable Seamark situated at the junction of Sands Lane and South Promenade, Hornsea (**TA 209 479**).

You will probably remember for a very long time the trackbeds of the old railway lines, the canals, the abbey and the castle, the natural history of the Longdendale Valley and the engineering at the Woodhead Tunnel. There will have been cups of tea, the occasional pint or glass of wine and friendly B&Bs. These

Stage 4: Selby to Hornsea

small, yet intense, moments are what makes long-distance cycle touring such a joy. Yet more than this, it is the people that you will have met along the way that will have really brought this four-day ride to life. From Merseyside to Humberside you will have encountered friendly and warm-hearted folk, who will have stopped you for a chat and wanted to hear the story of your TPT journey. The history, the landscape, the cycling and the people are what makes the TPT a fantastic ride and you've done it. The Seamark marks the conclusion of the journey. Treat yourself to a bag of fresh fish and chips from Sullivans – you've definitely earned them – and while you look out across the North Sea you may catch yourself dreaming of your next big trip. Will it be Lands End to John O'Groats or London to Vienna?

The Trans Pennine Trail artwork at Hornsea signifies the end is in sight.

RESOURCES

ACCOMMODATION

Listed west to east.

HOTELS AND B&Bs
Bay Tree House
Marine Gate
Southport
Merseyside
PR9 0HD
01704 510 555
SD 339 180

The Ambassador Townhouse
13 Bath Street
Southport
Merseyside
PR9 0DP
01704 543 998
SD 336 175

Bowden Lodge Hotel
18 Albert Road
Southport
Merseyside
PR9 0LE
01704 539 112
SD 342 179

Adelphi Guest House
39 Bold Street
Southport
Merseyside
PR9 0ED
01704 544 947
SD 336 176

Ramada Plaza
Marine Lake
Southport Promenade
Southport
Merseyside
PR9 0DZ
01704 516 220
SD 335 176

Resources

The New England
67 Bath Street
Southport
Merseyside
PR9 0ND
01704 500 643
SD 340 180

Carleton House
17 Alexandra Road
Southport
Merseyside
PR9 0NB
01704 538 035
SD 342 180

Talbot Hotel
23–25 Portland Street
Southport
Merseyside
PR8 1LR
01704 533 975
SD 335 168

Royal Clifton
The Promenade
Southport
Merseyside
PR8 1RB
08457 76 76 76
01704 533 771
SD 333 172

Britannia Prince of Wales
Lord Street
Southport
Merseyside
PR8 1JS
0871 474 2755
SD 334 170

Scarisbrick Hotel
239 Lord Street
Southport
Merseyside
PR8 1NZ
0871 222 7006
SD 334 172

Resources

The Vincent
98 Lord Street
Southport
Merseyside
PR8 1JR
01704 883 800
SD 336 173

Hale Village Guest House
11 Church End
Hale Village
Hale
Liverpool
Merseyside
L24 4AX
0151 425 5104
SJ 469 822

Church End Farm
5 Church End
Hale Village
Near Liverpool
Merseyside
L24 4AX
0151 425 4273
SJ 469 822

Corus Widnes Hotel
75 Cronton Lane
Widnes
Cheshire
WA8 9AR
0844 736 8610
SJ 508 883

The Mersey Hotel
146–148 Mersey Road
Widnes
Cheshire
WA8 0DT
0151 420 6924
SJ 511 838

Resources

Best Western Everglades Park Hotel
Derby Road
Widnes
Cheshire
WA8 3UJ
0151 495 5500
SJ 527 878

The Robins Guest House
1 Bargyloo Cottage
Warrington Road
Bold Heath
Warrington
Cheshire
WA8 3XW
01925 790 154
07724 965 015
SJ 546 889

Travelodge Warrington
Kendrick/Leigh Street
Warrington
Cheshire
WA1 1UZ
0871 984 6180
SJ 601 884

Patten Arms Hotel
Parker Street
Warrington
Cheshire
WA1 1LS
01925 636 602
SJ 600 878

Holiday Inn Warrington
Woolston Grange Avenue
Warrington
Cheshire
WA1 4PX
0871 942 9087
SJ 659 892

Heathside Guest House
12 Froghall Lane
Warrington
Cheshire
WA2 7JR
01925 631 774
SJ 601 885

Resources

Ramada Encore Warrington
Aston Avenue
Birchwood Business Park
Warrington
Cheshire
WA3 6ZN
01925 847 050
SJ 655 919

De Vere Village Warrington Hotel
Daresbury
Warrington
Cheshire
WA4 4BB
0844 980 2360
SJ 572 817

Best Western Fir Grove Hotel
Knutsford Old Road
Warrington
Cheshire
WA4 2LD
0845 776 7676
01925 267 471
SJ 630 869

Hotel Villaggio
5–9 Folly Lane
Warrington
Cheshire
WA5 0LZ
01925 630 106
SJ 598 892

The Lymm Hotel
Whitbarrow Road
Lymm
Cheshire
WA13 9AQ
0844 879 9047
SJ 679 875

Statham Lodge Country House Hotel
Warrington Road
Statham
Lymm
Cheshire
WA13 9BP
01925 752 205
SJ 668 876

Resources

Ash Farm Country Guest House
Ash Farm
Park Lane
Little Bollington
Altrincham
Cheshire
WA14 4TJ
0161 929 9290
SJ 730 871

Mercure Altrincham Bowdon Hotel
Langham Road
Bowdon
Altrincham
Cheshire
WA14 2HT
0161 928 7121
SJ 765 866

Cornbroke Guesthouse
15 Manchester Road
Altrincham
Cheshire
WA14 4RG
0161 941 2789
SJ 766 885

Premier Inn
Manchester Road
Altrincham
Cheshire
WA14 4PH
0871 527 8738
SJ 766 884

Sugar Brook Farm Bed and Breakfast
Mobberley Road
Ashley
Altrincham
Cheshire
WA14 3QB
0161 928 0879
SJ 772 830

Resources

The Thistlewood
203 Urmston Lane
Stretford
Manchester
Greater Manchester
M32 9EF
0161 865 3611
SJ 784 943

Britannia Country House Hotel
Palatine Road
Didsbury
Manchester
Greater Manchester
M20 2WG
0871 474 2755
SJ 836 910

The Waterside Hotel
Wilmslow Road
Didsbury
Manchester
Greater Manchester
M20 5WZ
0161 445 0225
SJ 854 896

Eleven Didsbury Park
Didsbury Park
Didsbury Village
Manchester
Greater Manchester
M20 5LH
0161 448 7711
SJ 849 905

Premier Inn Manchester West Didsbury
Christie Fields Business Park
Derwent Avenue
Manchester
Greater Manchester
M21 7QS
0871 527 8722
SJ 829 921

Resources

Premier Inn
Churchgate
Stockport
Greater Manchester
SK1 1YG
0871 527 9040
SJ 898 903

Henrys Hotel
205–206 Buxton Road
Davenport
Stockport
Greater Manchester
SK2 7AE
0161 292 0202
SJ 904 883

Alma Lodge Hotel
149 Buxton Road
Stockport
Greater Manchester
SK2 6EL
0161 483 4431
SJ 903 885

Britannia Hotel Stockport
Dialstone Lane
Offerton
Stockport
Greater Manchester
SK2 6AG
0871 474 2755
SJ 911 891

Innkeeper's Lodge
271 Wellington Road North
Heaton Chapel
Stockport
Greater Manchester
SK4 5BP
0845 112 6027
SJ 883 920

Resources

Premier Inn Hyde
Stockport Road
Mottram
Hyde
Cheshire
SK14 3AU
0871 527 8712
SJ 983 952

De Vere Village Hotel
Captain Clarke Road
Hyde
Cheshire
SK14 4QG
0844 980 8034
01239 758 087
SJ 939 964

Windy Harbour Farm Hotel
Woodhead Road
Glossop
Derbyshire
SK13 7QE
01457 853 107
SK 037 958

Wayside Cottage B&B
106 Padfield Main Road
Padfield
Glossop
Derbyshire
SK13 1ET
01457 866495
SK 031 963

Birds Nest Cottage Guest House
40–42 Primrose Lane
Glossop
Derbyshire
SK13 8EW
01457 853 478
07711 353 696
SK 024 939

Resources

Peakdale Lodge
49-53 High Street East
Glossop
Derbyshire
SK13 8PN
01457 854109
SK 036 940

Hikers and Bikers
105 Station Road
Hadfield
Glossop
Debyshire
SK13 1AA
01457 854672
SK 023 961

Avondale Guesthouse
28 Woodhead Road
Glossop
Derbyshire
SK13 7RH
01457 853132
07784 764969
SK 037 948

Ye Olde Mustard Pot
Mortimer Road
Midhopestones
Sheffield
S36 4GW
01226 761155
SE 219 062

Cubley Hall
Mortimer Road
Penistone
Sheffield
South Yorkshire
S36 9DF
01226 766086
SE 244 021

Carr House Barn
Royd Lane
Millhouse Green
Penistone
S36 9NY
01226 762917
SE 217 037

Resources

Travellers Inn
23 Green Road
Dodworth
Barnsley
S75 3RR
01226 284173
SE 313 050

New Country Inn
The Fairway
Elmhirst Lane
Dodworth
Barnsley
South Yorkshire
S75 4LS
0871 200 2289
SE 308 056

The Old Vicarage
33 Barnsley Road
Cawthorne
Barnsley
South Yorks
S75 4HW
01226 790063
SE 286 079

Wortley Cottage Guest House
Park Avenue
Wortley
Sheffield
S35 7DB
0114 288 1864
SK 307 994

Tankersley Manor
Church Lane
Tankersley
Barnsley
South Yorkshire
S75 3DQ
01226 744700
SK 343 994

Resources

Delf Cottage
Houndhill Lane
Worsbrough
Barnsley
South Yorkshire
S70 6TX
01226 282 430
SE 336 042

The Old Coach House
255 Doncaster Road
Stairfoot
Barnsley
South Yorkshire
S70 3RH
01226 290 612
SE 365 057

Premier Inn
Barnsley (Dearne Valley)
Meadow Gate
Valley Park
Dearne Valley
Wombwell
Barnsley
South Yorkshire
S73 0UN
0871 527 8050
SE 413 024

The Lord Conyers Hotel
Old Road
Conisbrough
Doncaster
South Yorkshire
DN12 3LZ
01709 863 254
SK 507 985

Best Western Pastures Hotel
Pastures Road
Mexborough
Doncaster
South Yorkshire
S64 0JJ
08457 76 76 76
01709 577707
SE 493 002

Resources

Rock Farm
Hooton Pagnell
South Yorkshire
DN5 7BT
01977 642200
07785 916186
SE 484 081

Townfields Hotel
60 Thorne Road
Doncaster
South Yorkshire
DN1 2JW
01302 342 972
SE 583 036

The Caribbean Hotel
87–89 Thorne Road
Doncaster
South Yorkshire
DN1 2ES
01302 364 605
SE 582 036

Danum Hotel
High Street
Doncaster
South Yorkshire
DN1 1DN
01302 342 261
SE 575 032

The Regent Hotel
Regent Square
Doncaster
South Yorkshire
DN1 2DS
01302 364 180
SE 580 031

Premier Inn
Doncaster Central
High Fishergate
Doncaster
South Yorkshire
DN1 1QZ
0871 527 8302
SE 575 035

Resources

Balmoral Guest House
129 Thorne Road
Doncaster
South Yorkshire
DN2 5BH
01302 364 385
SE 587 041

The Wheatley Hotel
Thorne Road
Wheatley Hills
Doncaster
South Yorkshire
DN2 5DR
01302 364 092
SE 600 053

The Lodge
The Olive Bar and Grill
1–3 Station Road
Barnby Dun
Doncaster
South Yorkshire
DN3 1HA
01302 891 403
SE 618 088

Woodborough Hotel
2 Belle Vue Avenue
Doncaster
South Yorkshire
DN4 5DX
01302 361 381
SE 592 026

Holiday Inn
High Road
Warmsworth
Doncaster
South Yorkshire
DN4 9UX
0871 423 4878
SE 546 006

Resources

Restover Lodge Doncaster
Ten Pound Walk
Doncaster
South Yorkshire
DN4 5HX
01302 761 050
SE 577 021

Holiday Inn Express
Catesby Business Park
First Point
Doncaster
South Yorkshire
DN4 8SJ
01302 314 100
SE 583 015

The Brewers Arms Hotel
10 Pontefract Road
Snaith
East Riding of Yorkshire
DN14 9JS
01405 862 404
SE 641 220

Royal Oak Inn
Main Street
Hirst Courtney
Selby
North Yorkshire
YO8 8QP
01757 270 633
SE 609 246

Hagthorpe House
Brackenholme
Selby
North Yorkshire
YO8 6EL
01757 638 867
SE 700 300

Berewick House
Park Lane
Barlow
Selby
North Yorkshire
YO8 8EW
01757 617 051
SE 649 284

Resources

New Country Inns
Selby Hotel
Oakney Wood Drive
Selby
North Yorkshire
YO8 8LZ
08712 003 363
SE 616 304

Hazeldene Guest House
32–34 Brook Street
Doncaster Road
Selby
North Yorkshire
YO8 4AR
01757 704 809
SE 610 320

Maypole Farm B&B
14 Wistowgate
Cawood
Selby
North Yorkshire
YO8 3SH
01757 268 849
SE 577 373

Dove Cottage B&B
Back Lane
Drax
Selby
North Yorkshire
YO8 8NY
01757 617103
07885 205 693
SE 670 265

South Newlands Farm B&B
Selby Road
Riccall
York
North Yorkshire
YO19 6QR
01757 248 203
SE 637 369

Resources

Dove Cottage near Selby, a comfortable, family-run bed and breakfast near Selby. (Photo: Brian Thornton)

Mercure Hull Royal Hotel
170 Ferensway
Kingston upon Hull
Humberside
East Riding of Yorkshire
HU1 3UF
01482 325 087
TA 092 287

Portland Hotel
Paragon Street
Kingston upon Hull
East Riding of Yorkshire
HU1 3JP
01482 213 460
TA 094 287

Ibis Hotel
Osbourne Street
Ferensway
Kingston upon Hull
East Riding of Yorkshire
HU1 2NL
0871 663 0628
TA 094 286

Resources

Holiday Inn
Hull Marina
Castle Street North
Kingston upon Hull
East Riding of Yorkshire
HU1 2BX
0871 423 4878
TA 095 283

Kingston Theatre Hotel
1–2 Kingston Square
Kingston upon Hull
East Riding of Yorkshire
01482 225 828
HU2 8DA
TA 096 291

The Admiral Guest House
234 Boulevard
Kingston upon Hull
East Riding of Yorkshire
HU3 3ED
01482 329 664
TA 080 278

Pearson Park Hotel
70–72 Pearson Park
Kingston upon Hull
East Riding of Yorkshire
HU5 2TQ
01482 343 043
TA 087 306

Acorn Guest House
719 Beverley Road
Kingston upon Hull
East Riding of Yorkshire
HU6 7JN
01482 853 248
07549 960 325
TA 083 323

Park Lodge Guest House
122 Summergangs Road
Kingston upon Hull
East Riding of Yorkshire
HU8 8LP
01482 797 144
TA 118 308

Resources

Premier Inn
Tower Street
Kingston upon Hull
East Riding of Yorkshire
HU9 1TQ
0871 527 8534
TA 104 286

Redcliffe House B&B
Redcliff Road
Hessle
East Riding of Yorkshire
HU13 0HA
01482 648 655
TA 027 255

West Carlton Country Guest House
Carlton Road
Aldbrough
East Riding of Yorkshire
HU11 4RB
01964 527 724
TA 226 389

Sandhurst Guest House
3 Victoria Avenue
Hornsea
East Riding of Yorkshire
HU18 1NH
01964 534 653
TA 207 482

Albert and Victoria Guest House
2 Victoria Avenue
Hornsea
East Riding of Yorkshire
HU18 1NH
01964 533 310
TA 207 482

Acorn Lodge Guest House
31 New Road
Hornsea
East Riding of Yorkshire
HU18 1PG
01964 536 733
07968 026 616
TA 206 478

Resources

Admiralty Guest House
7 Marine Drive
Hornsea
East Riding of Yorkshire
HU18 1NJ
01964 536 414
TA 208 480

CAMPSITES
Willow Bank Holiday and Touring Park
Coastal Road
Ainsdale
Southport
Merseyside
PR8 3ST
01704 571 566
SD 309 107

Riverside Holiday Park
Southport New Road
Banks
Southport
Merseyside
PR9 8DF
01704 228 886
SD 403 194

Holly Bank Caravan Park
Warburton Bridge Road
Rixton
Warrington
Cheshire
WA3 6HU
0161 775 2842
SJ 693 905

Lymefield Farm Camp Site
Broadbottom
via Hyde
Cheshire
SK14 6AG
01457 764 626
SJ 996 935

Resources

Hayfield Camping
Kinder Road
Hayfield
Derbyshire
SK22 2LE
01663 745 394
SK 042 867

Ingfield Farm Camp Site
Ingbirchworth
Nr Penistone
South Yorkshire
S36 7GG
01226 767 938
SE 222 058

Ranah Stones Farm
Hazlehead
Crow Edge
Penistone
Sheffield
South Yorkshire
S36 4HJ
01226 370 345
SE 193 030

Paw Hill Farm
Fullshaw Cross
Penistone
Sheffield
South Yorkshire
S36 9FP
01226 763 196
SE 213 014

Woodland View Caravan Site
322 Barnsley Road
Hoylandswaine
Penistone
South Yorkshire
S36 7HA
01226 761 906
SE 267 047

Resources

Greensprings Touring Park
Rockley Abbey Farm
Rockley Lane
Worsbrough, Barnsley
South Yorkshire
S75 3DS
01226 288 298
SE 336 019

Hatfield Water Park
Old Thorne Road
Hatfield
Doncaster
South Yorkshire
DN7 6EQ
01302 841 572
SE 670 100

Fisherman Inn
Hayfield Lane
Auckley
Doncaster
South Yorkshire
DN9 3NP
01302 863 699
SK 644 997

Elmstone Farm
Applehurst Lane
Thorpe In Balne
Doncaster
South Yorkshire
DN6 0DZ
01302 885 478
SE 595 108

The Ranch Caravan Park
Cliffe Common
Selby
North Yorkshire
YO8 6EF
01757 638 984
SE 665 340

Resources

Royal Oak Inn Camp Site
Main Street
Hirst Courtney
Selby
North Yorkshire
YO8 8QP
01757 270633
SE 610 246

Moss Hagg Farm
Selby Common
Selby
North Yorkshire
YO8 3RE
01757 703 279
SE 578 333

The Sloop Inn
Main Road
Temple Hirst
Selby
North Yorkshire
YO8 8QN
01757 270267
SE 606 248

South Newlands Farm Campsite
Selby Road
Riccall
York
North Yorkshire
YO19 6QR
01757 248203
SE 637 369

Approach Farm Caravan and Camp Site
Hollicarrs
Escrick
York
North Yorkshire
YO19 6EE
01757 248 250
SE 628 391

Resources

The Rancher
Barrow Road
Barton upon Humber
North Lincolnshire
DN18 6DA
01652 633 171
TA 040 217

Burton Constable Holiday Park
Old Lodges
Sproatley
Kingston upon Hull
East Yorkshire
HU11 4LN
01964 562 508
TA 189 366

White Cottage Camping
Hull Road
Seaton
Nr Hornsea
East Yorkshire
HU11 5RN
07813 205087
TA 197 448

Northorpe Certificated Site
Atwick Road
Hornsea
East Yorkshire
HU18 1EJ
01964 534063
TA 195 487

YOUTH HOSTELS
YHA Liverpool
25 Tabley Street
Wapping
Liverpool
Merseyside
L1 8EE
0845 371 9527
SJ 341 896

Resources

YHA Manchester
Potato Wharf
Castlefield
Manchester
Greater Manchester
M3 4NB
0845 371 9647
SJ 832 977

Hatters Hostel
Hilton Chambers
15 Hilton Street
Manchester
Greater Manchester
M1 1JJ
0161 236 4414
SJ 844 984

YHA Crowden
Crowden-in-Longdendale
Glossop
Derbyshire
SK13 1HZ
0845 371 9113
SK 071 993

YHA Beverley Friary
Friar's Lane
Beverley
East Riding of Yorkshire
HU17 0DF
0845 371 9004
TA 038 392

CYCLE REPAIR SHOPS

Listed west to east.

Southport Cycle Centre
Southport Railway Station
London Street
Southport
Merseyside
PR8 1BE
01704 500 996
SD 338 171

Resources

Mosscrop Cycles
78 Bispham Road
Southport
Merseyside
PR9 7DF
01704 228 805
SD 358 171

Birkdale Cycles
272 Liverpool Road
Birkdale
Southport
Merseyside
PR8 4PE
01704 567 351
SD 328 141

Crays
207 Liverpool Road North
Maghull
Merseyside
L31 2HH
0151 526 9566
SD 373 030

Oban Cycles Anfield
59 Breck Road
Anfield
Liverpool
Merseyside
L4 2QX
0151 263 6332
SJ 356 945

Oban Cycles Walton
234 County Road
Walton
Liverpool
Merseyside
L4 5PJ
0151 523 1523
SJ 357 946

Resources

Quinns Bike Centre
383/385 Edge Lane
Liverpool
Merseyside
L7 9LQ
0151 228 6262
SJ 383 907

Hobson Cycles
62 Walton Vale
Walton
Liverpool
L9 2BU
0151 281 8941
SJ 364 966

Cyclehouse
Unit 1
Portland Trade Park
Buckley Street
Warrington
Cheshire
WA2 7NS
01925 576 555
SJ 604 887

John Geddes Cycles
43 Widnes Road
Widnes
Cheshire
WA8 6AZ
0151 420 7797
SJ 516 858

Cyclelife Lymm
1 Birchbrook Road
Lymm
Cheshire
WA13 9RR
01925 753 424
SJ 698 882

Resources

Cyclelife Sale
67 Cross Street
Sale
Manchester
Greater Manchester
M33 7HF
0161 962 3037
SJ 786 923

Cycle Surgery
Unit 1
751-807 Princess Parkway
Princess Park
Didsbury
Manchester
Greater Manchester
M20 2ZE
0161 448 4444
SJ 829 917

Woodsons Cycles
85c Castle Street
Edgeley
Stockport
Greater Manchester
SK3 9AR
0161 480 8725
SJ 889 894

Wills Wheels Cycle Shop and Repairs
482 Manchester Road
Heaton Chapel
Stockport
Greater Manchester
SK4 5DL
0161 432 4936
SJ 882 925

The Bike Shop
111 Stockport Road
Marple
Stockport
Greater Manchester
SK6 6AF
0161 427 8505
SJ 955 886

Resources

Bicycle Smithy
189 London Road
Hazel Grove
Stockport
Greater Manchester
SK7 4HJ
0161 483 3313
SJ 920 870

Halfords
Unit 11
Wren Nest Retail Park
Glossop
Derbyshire
SK13 8GN
01457 891010
SK 029 941

High Peak Cycles
2 Smithy Fold
Glossop
Derbyshire
SK13 8DD
01457 861535
SK 035 940

RaceScene
210–212 Upper Sheffield Road
Barnsley
South Yorkshire
S70 4PG
01226 292 111
SE 350 054

Halfords
Dryden Road
Harborough Hill Road
Barnsley
South Yorkshire
S71 1JE
01226 730 640
SE 351 068

Resources

Halfords
Cortonwood
Brampton
Barnsley
South Yorskhire
S73 0TB
01226 344010
SE 406 013

Conisbrough Scooters and Cycles
72 Old Road
Conisbrough
Doncaster
South Yorkshire
DN12 3LU
0845 508 7928
SK 504 984

Don Valley Cycles
10 Chequer Road
Doncaster
South Yorkshire
DN1 2AF
01302 769531
SE 579 028

Cycle Supreme
7/9 Bennetthorpe
Doncaster
South Yorkshire
DN4 8SN
01302 857906
SK 572 997

Halfords
Northbridge Road
Doncaster
South Yorkshire
DN5 9AN
01302 767030
SE 569 038

Halfords
Unit 2C
Bawtry Road
Selby
North Yorkshire
YO8 8LY
01757 706214
SE 617 311

Resources

Selby Bike Centre
49 Gowthorpe
Selby
North Yorkshire
YO8 4HE
01757 702385
SE 612 323

Freetown Sports
70–76 Prospect Street
Kingston upon Hull
East Riding of Yorkshire
HU1 3RT
01482 589066
TA 093 290

Cliff Pratt Cycles
84–86 Spring Bank Hull
Kingston upon Hull
East Riding of Yorkshire
HU3 1AA
01482 228 293
TA 088 294

Halfords
Unit 2, St Andrews Quay
Kingston upon Hull
East Riding of Yorkshire
HU3 4SA
01482 210244
TA 073 269

Halfords
Clough Road
Kingston upon Hull
East Riding of Yorkshire
HU5 1SW
01482 447377

TA 094 313

FITNESS

Map My Ride, www.mapmyride.com
Bike Radar, www.bikeradar.com
Net Doctor, www.netdoctor.co.uk
Cycling and Weight Loss, www.weightlossresources.co.uk/logout/sport/cycling.htm
Real Buzz Cycle Training, www.realbuzz.com/cycling

Resources

GENERAL

Natural England, www.naturalengland.org.uk
Campaign to Protect Rural England, www.cpre.org.uk
Groundwork, www.groundwork.org.uk
Joint Nature Conservation Committee, www.jncc.defra.gov.uk
The Mammal Society, www.mammal.org.uk
Mersey Basin, www.merseybasin.org.uk
Sefton Coast, www.seftoncoast.org.uk
National Biodiversity Network, www.nbn.org.uk
Lancashire and North Merseyside Wildlife Trust, www.lancswt.org.uk
St. John Ambulance First Aid, www.sja.org.uk

GENERAL CYCLING

Benefits of Cycling NHS, www.nhs.uk/Livewell/fitness/Pages/Cycling.aspx
Bike 4 Life, www.nhs.uk/change4life/Pages/bike-for-life.aspx
Sustrans, www.sustrans.org.uk
CTC, National Cycling Charity, www.ctc.org.uk
Warm Showers, www.warmshowers.org
British Cycling, www.britishcycling.org.uk
London Cycling Campaign, www.lcc.org.uk
Why Cycle, www.whycycle.co.uk
Hull Cycle Streets, www.hull.cyclestreets.net
Cyclecraft, www.cyclecraft.co.uk
Tandem Club, www.tandem-club.org.uk
The Tricycle Association, www.tricycleassociation.org.uk
Bikeability, www.bikeability.dft.gov.uk
Audax, www.aukweb.net
Life Cycle, www.lifecycleuk.org.uk
Cycle Training, www.cycletraining.co.uk
Cyclesense Bike Shop, www.cyclesense.co.uk
Russell's Bike Shed, www.russellsbicycleshed.co.uk

MAPS

Trans Pennine Trail Scale 1: 50,000 Official route maps
Map 1 West: Irish Sea – Yorkshire, ISBN 987-0-953-22777-8
Map 2 Central: Derbyshire – Yorkshire, ISBN 978-0-953-22778-5
Map 3 East: Yorkshire – North Sea, ISBN 978-0-953-22779-2
Ordnance Survey Landranger Series Scale 1:50,000
1. Ordnance Survey Sheet 108: Liverpool
ISBN 978-0-319-22838-8
2. Ordnance Survey Sheet 109: Manchester

Resources

ISBN 978-0-319-23155-5
3. Ordnance Survey Sheet 110: Sheffield and Huddersfield
ISBN 978-0-319-22944-6
4. Ordnance Survey Sheet 111: Sheffield and Doncaster
ISBN 978-0-319-22935-1
5. Ordnance Survey Sheet 105: York and Selby
ISBN 978-0-319-22945-3
6. Ordnance Survey Sheet 106: Market Weighton
ISBN 978-0319-22952-1
7. Ordnance Survey Sheet 107: Kingston upon Hull
ISBN 978-0-319-22454-6

MOBILE CYCLE MECHANICS

Listed west to east.

Barry's Mobile Bicycle Maintenance
07738 114243
Knowsley and Merseyside

Dart
0800 110 5829
The Wirral, Liverpool and West Cheshire

RevolveMCR
07939 062600
Manchester within the M60

Cycle Tech Tameside
07980 693310
Glossop, Hadfield, Longdendale, Glossopdale

Bicycle Buddy
07585 904818
South Yorkshire, Doncaster, Barnsley, Rotherham

Russells Bicycle Shed
07557 410553
Dunford Bridge to Old Moor RSPB, Dearne Valley, Rotherham

Repair 2 Ride
07957 026262
Selby, Brough, North Ferriby, Hull.

Resources

NUTRITION

Cycle Route, www.cycle-route.com/cycle-guides/Cycling_Nutrition-8.html
Bicycling, www.bicycling.com/tags/bicycling-nutrition
Crispin Bennett, www.crispinbennett.freedomnames.co.uk/Nutrition.htm
Bicycle Source, www.bicyclesource.com/body/nutrition
Road Cycling UK, www.roadcyclinguk.com/riding/nutrition-five-top-tips.html
Kate Percy, *Go Faster Food* (Random: London, 2009)
Nancy Clark and Jenny Hegmann, *The Cyclist's Food Guide* (Sports Nutrition: USA, 2011)
Gale Bernhardt, *Training Plans for Cyclists* (Velo: USA, 2009)
Suzanne Girard Eberle, *Endurance Sports Nutrition* (Human Kinetics: USA, 2007)
Jane Griffin, *Nutrition for Cyclists* (Crowood Press, 2014)

TAXIS FROM HORNSEA

Costello Taxis
141a Askew Avenue, Kingston upon Hull, East Riding of Yorkshire, HU4 6NH
01482 656 565
TA 058 278

535353 Taxis
44 Eastgate, Hornsea, East Riding of Yorkshire, HU18 1LW
01964 535 353
TA 204 480

Hull Cars
124 Anlaby Road, Kingston upon Hull, East Riding of Yorkshire, HU3 2JH
01482 828 282
TA 087 286

Star Taxis
2 Salisbury Avenue, Hornsea, East Riding of Yorkshire, HU18 1SX
01964 533 247
TA 204 467

TOURIST INFORMATION

Trans Pennine Trail, www.transpenninetrail.org.uk
East Peak Innovation Partnership, www.epip.org.uk
Visit England, www.visitengland.com
Visit Southport, www.visitsouthport.com
Visit Liverpool, www.visitliverpool.com
Visit Chester and Cheshire, www.visitchester.com

Resources

Visit Manchester, www.visitmanchester.com
Visit Derbyshire, www.visitderbyshire.co.uk
Welcome to Yorkshire, www.yorkshire.com
Visit Barnsley, www.visit-barnsley.com
Visit Hull and East Yorkshire, www.visithullandeastyorkshire.com
English Heritage, www.english-heritage.org.uk

TRAIN OPERATORS

Arriva Trains Wales, 0870 9000 773
2c, 0845 601 4873
Chiltern Railways, 08456 005 165
Cross Country, 0844 811 0124
East Coast, 08457 225 225
East Midlands Trains, 08457 125 678
Eurostar, 0844 822 5822
First Capital Connect, 0845 026 4700
First Great Western, 08457 000 125
First Hull Trains, 08450 710 222
First Trans Pennine Express, 0845 600 1674
Gatwick Express, 0845 850 1530
Grand Central Rail, 0845 603 4852
Greater Anglia, 0845 600 7245
Heathrow Connect, 0845 678 6975
Heathrow Express, 0845 600 1515
Island Line Trains, 0845 6000 650
London Midland, 0844 811 0133
London Overground, 0845 601 4867
Merseyrail, 0151 702 2071
National Rail, 08457 48 49 50
Northern Rail, 0845 000 0125
Scotrail, 0845 601 5929
Southern, 08451 27 29 20
South Eastern, 08451 000 2222
South Western Trains, 0845 6000 650
Stansted Express, 0845 600 7245
Train Tracker, 0871 200 49 50
Train Tracker Text Journey Planning Functions, 84950
Virgin Trains, 0871 977 4222

INDEX OF VILLAGES, TOWNS AND LANDMARKS

Listed west to east.

Southport 23, 24, 25, 26, 27
Ainsdale-on-Sea 25
Downholland Moss 27
Maghull 27
Aintree Station 31
Walton 31
West Derby 30, 31
Knotty Ash 31
Speke 31
Hale 31, 32, 34
Pickerings Pasture Nature Reserve 32, 33, 36
Spike Island, Widnes 33
Ferry Tavern Public House 34, 35
Wilderspool 36
Latchford Locks 37, 39, 40, 41
Lymm 41, 43, 45
Carrington Lane 45
Stretford 46
Jackson's Boat Pub 46, 47
Northenden 48
Stockport 43, 48, 49, 50
Lancashire Hill 49
Reddish Vale Visitor Centre 49, 51
Haughton Dale 52
Hyde 52
Broadbottom 52
Charlesworth 52
Melandra Roman Fort 54
Hadfield 54, 55
Woodhead Tunnel 55, 56, 60, 61, 63, 64
Woodhead Reservoir 56, 57
Gallows Moss 64, 66, 68
Dunford Bridge 62, 63, 64, 68

Penistone 68
Oxspring 68, 69, 70
Tankersley Manor 70, 71
Wentworth Castle 70, 71, 73, 77
Dodworth Bottom 83, 86
Worsbrough 73, 75
RSPB Old Moor 73, 75, 76, 77, 78
Harlington 78
Conisbrough 78, 79, 80, 81, 82
Bentley 83
Tilts 83
Thorpe 83
Braithwaite 83
Gowdall 85
Snaith 85
RAF Burn 86, 87, 88, 89
Selby 84, 87, 88, 89, 90, 91, 93
Barmby Barrage 94
Knedlington 94, 95
Howden 95, 97
Kilpin 95
Saltmarshe 95
Yokefleet 95
Blacktoft 95
Weighton Lock 96, 97
Broomfleet 97
Elloughton 99
Welton 99
North Ferriby 99
Humber Bridge 99, 100, 101, 102, 103, 104
Hessle 104
Kingston upon Hull 99
Oubrough 106
Hornsea 106, 107, 108